FREUD AND MAN'S SOUL

Bruno Bettelheim

PENGUIN BOOKS

PENGUIN BOOKS

Published by the Penguin Group
Penguin Books Ltd, 27 Wrights Lane, London W8 5TZ, England
Viking Penguin, a division of Penguin Books USA Inc.
375 Hudson Street, New York, New York 10014, USA
Penguin Books Australia Ltd, Ringwood, Victoria, Australia
Penguin Books Canada Ltd, 2801 John Street, Markham, Ontario, Canada L3R 1B4
Penguin Books (NZ) Ltd, 182–190 Wairau Road, Auckland 10, New Zealand

Penguin Books Ltd, Registered Offices: Harmondsworth, Middlesex, England

First published in the USA by Alfred A. Knopf 1983
First published in Great Britain by Chatto & Windus · The Hogarth Press 1983
Published in Pelican Books 1989
Reprinted in Penguin Books 1991
1 3 5 7 9 10 8 6 4 2

Printed in England by Clays Ltd, St Ives plc

SB 2772 (2) /4.99. 4.91

IAL
(Bet

Bruno Bettelheim, one of the world's most distinguished psychoanalysts, was the founder of the Orthogenic School at Chicago University and until his retirement in 1973 was its Director. Born in Vienna in 1903, he received his doctorate at the University of Vienna. During the Second World War, he was interned in the concentration camps of Dachau and Buchenwald, and it is about this that he wrote in *The Informed Heart*. After moving to the USA he became Professor of T...

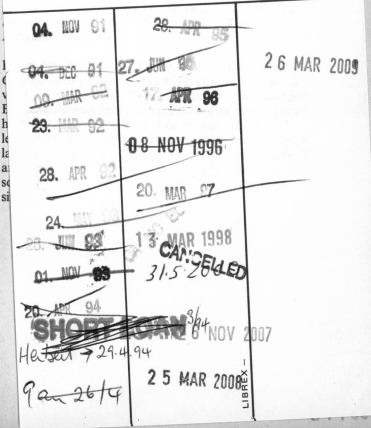

Psychoanalysis is in essence
a cure through love.

FREUD, *in a letter to Jung*

Preface

The English translations of Freud's writings are seriously defective in important respects and have led to erroneous conclusions, not only about Freud the man but also about psychoanalysis. This applies even to the authoritative *Standard Edition of the Complete Psychological Works of Sigmund Freud*. After reading the criticisms of this translation that I present in this book, the reader may well ask why I have waited so long to publish them, and why others have not made similar criticisms long ago. Obviously, I cannot answer the second question with any certainty, but the reasons for my own reluctance may suggest why others too have hesitated to criticize the translations.

Conversations with friends have disclosed that many who, like myself, are native German-speakers, and emigrated to the United States in the middle of their lives, are quite dissatisfied with the way Freud's works have been rendered in English. The number of inadequacies and downright errors in the translations is enormous; merely to correct the more blatant ones would be a tremendous task, and the decision where to begin and what to concentrate on would be extremely difficult. But the reluctance to discuss openly the inadequacy of the available translations has been ultimately due, I believe, to much deeper psychological reservations.

Most of the translations were completed in Freud's lifetime, and were accepted or, at the very least, condoned by him. The chief editor of the *Standard Edition* was one of his followers whom Freud personally entrusted with the translation of some of his works; and the co-editor was his daughter Anna, the person closest to Freud in the last years of his life and his chosen successor. Under these circumstances, criticizing the translations has come to seem almost like criticizing the venerated master himself. And there has been a general shying away from doing so, accompanied by the persistent hope that others—ideally, Freud's chosen heirs—would undertake this onerous but very necessary task.

This has been my own hope for nearly forty years. I know that others much closer than I to the editors of the *Standard Edition* have broached the problem and proposed various remedies, such as adding a twenty-fifth volume of corrective glossaries. All such suggestions have proved unacceptable to the publisher.

Most of the people who lived in Freud's Vienna, and became familiar with his thought in that place and time, either have died or are now in their seventies or eighties, approaching the end of their lives. If, therefore, the mistranslations with which the *Standard Edition* unfortunately abounds are ever to be corrected by someone who shared Freud's cultural background and is closely acquainted with the language as Freud himself used it, it must be done now. This is why I have at last overcome the reluctance that I have felt for so long.

Time has not allowed me anything approaching a complete discussion of the many mistranslations—something that would in any case be far beyond my capabilities. And deciding what to focus on has not been easy, especially since so many widely held ideas about Freud the man, his life, and aspects of his thought are based on misunderstandings that have resulted from defective presentations of his thought in translation, even faulty renderings of quite simple remarks he made about himself.

In a brief memoir Freud wrote when he was eighty, he relates an experience he had more than thirty years earlier, on the occasion of a trip to Athens, as he stood on the Acropolis ("A Disturbance of Memory on the Acropolis"). This memoir reveals much about Freud: about his feelings during his school years, about his relationship with his father, about his background. In the final sentence Freud says that after he had succeeded in analyzing the deeper meaning of his experience on the Acropolis, he was frequently visited by the memory of it—which was not surprising, since he himself was now old, needful of forbearance (an obvious reference to his terminal illness), and no longer able to travel. Freud's exact words are: "*Und jetzt werden Sie sich nicht mehr verwundern, dass mich die Erinnerung an das Erlebnis auf der Akropolis so oft heimsucht....*" The word he uses here to refer to the frequent reappearance of this recollection, *heimsuchen*—"to visit"—is fraught with special meaning, because in Catholic Vienna the *Maria Heimsuchung* was (and still is) an important religious holiday, celebrating the visit of the Virgin Mary to Elizabeth, an event depicted in many famous paintings and sculptures with which Freud had become well acquainted in the travels he could now no longer undertake. And just as Mary learned on this visit something of profound importance about herself, so too did Freud's memory, after he successfully analyzed it, reveal to him things of greatest personal significance. His choice of the word *heimsucht* suggests this.

At the beginning of the essay, where Freud first states that this memory reasserted itself frequently, and mentions that initially he did not understand why, he uses the expression "*tauchte immer wieder auf.*" *Auftauchen* means, literally, "to surface" (out of deep water), but it is also used more broadly to refer to anything that appears suddenly or abruptly. That within this essay Freud employs these two quite different words to name a single phenomenon is an example of his masterly use of language. Before he analyzes the recurring memory, he refers to it with a word that connotes a sudden appearance out of unknown depths, suggesting emergence from the unconscious. After he analyzes it, and after the reader knows how deeply meaningful this memory is and why, Freud uses a word that alludes to a profoundly revealing event, the Visitation.

In the *Standard Edition*, the final sentence of this essay is translated: "And now you will no longer wonder that the recollection of this incident on the Acropolis should have troubled me so often. . . ." This mistranslation has been the occasion of some quite elaborate speculations about Freud's attitude toward his background, based on the assumption that he said this memory often "troubled" him. But he said nothing of the sort, remarking merely that it *visited* him often, and employing a word that, because of its ancient religious associations, suggests something of deepest import.

This is but one relatively minor example of how defective translation can lead, and has led, to erroneous conclusions about Freud—and I offer it to show why I have been tempted to discuss here all the many inadequate translations that have caused a variety of misconceptions about Freud and about the nature of psychoanalysis. But, as I have said above, a truly comprehensive study would be a task of such magnitude that I have not dared to attempt it. I have instead decided to concentrate on two smaller tasks: to correct the mistranslations of some of the most important psychoanalytic concepts; and to show how deeply humane a person Freud was, that he was a humanist in the best sense of the word. His greatest concern was with man's innermost being, to which he most frequently referred through the use of a metaphor—man's soul—because the word "soul" evokes so many emotional connotations. It is the greatest shortcoming of the current English versions of his works that they give no hint of this.

I have discussed the problem of the English translations of Freud's writings with students and friends over many years, and I have received so many helpful suggestions that it would be impossible to mention them all here. But I wish at least to acknowledge gratefully those given me by Dr. Paul Kramer, Dr. Richard Sterba, Trude Weisskopf, and Dr. Henry von Witzleben.

As so often in the past, many thanks are due to Joyce Jack for her sensitive and careful editing of the original manuscript of this book. Robert Gottlieb was so kind as to give it its final form, for which I am most grateful. Last but not least, I wish to thank Theron Raines for his valuable suggestions, and most of all for his encouragement, without which the book might never have been finished.

Most of the passages from Freud quoted here are taken from the *Standard Edition*. All unattributed translations are my own.

B.B.

FREUD AND MAN'S SOUL

I

As a child born into a middle-class, assimilated Jewish family in Vienna, I was raised and educated in an environment that was in many respects identical with the one that had formed Freud's background. The culture that was transmitted to me in my home, then in secondary school, and, finally, at the University of Vienna, had changed very little since Freud's student days, fifty years earlier. So it was natural that from the time I began to think on my own I read Freud. After studying his earlier works, I eagerly read his new ones as they appeared, from *Beyond the Pleasure Principle* (1920) and *The Ego and the Id* (1923) through all the later essays, in which his ideas reached their fullest development. Understanding Freud's writings was considerably facilitated by my thus being able to follow his ideas as he completed the edifice of psychoanalysis, which he had begun a few years before I was born. It was also facilitated by my being in analysis myself and by my study of psychoanalysis in the same unique Viennese cultural climate in which Freud worked and thought. When, in middle age, I was fortunate enough to be permitted to start a new life in the United States, and began to read and discuss psychoanalytic writings in English, I discovered that reading Freud in English translation leads to quite different impressions from those I had formed when I read him in German. It became apparent to me that the English renditions of Freud's writings distort much of the essential humanism that permeates the originals.

In *The Interpretation of Dreams* (1900), which opened to our understanding not just the meaning of dreams but also the nature and power of the unconscious, Freud told about his arduous struggle to achieve ever greater self-awareness. In other books, he told why he felt it necessary for the rest of us to do the same. In a way, all his writings are gentle, persuasive, often brilliantly worded intimations that we, his readers, would benefit from a similar spiritual journey of self-discovery. Freud showed us how the soul could become aware of itself. To become acquainted with the lowest depth of the soul—to explore whatever personal hell we may suffer from—is not an easy undertaking. Freud's findings and, even more, the way he presents them to us give us the confidence that this demanding and potentially dangerous voyage of self-discovery will result in our becoming more fully human, so that we may no longer be enslaved without knowing it to the dark forces that reside in us. By exploring and understanding the origins and the potency of these forces, we not only become much better able to cope with them but also gain a much deeper and more compassionate understanding of our fellow man. In his work and in his writings, Freud often spoke of the soul—of its nature and structure, its development, its attributes, how it reveals itself in all we do and dream. Unfortunately, nobody who reads him in English could guess this, because nearly all his many references to the soul, and to matters pertaining to the soul, have been excised in translation.

This fact, combined with the erroneous or inadequate

translation of many of the most important original concepts of psychoanalysis, makes Freud's direct and always deeply personal appeals to our common humanity appear to readers of English as abstract, depersonalized, highly theoretical, erudite, and mechanized—in short, "scientific"—statements about the strange and very complex workings of our mind. Instead of instilling a deep feeling for what is most human in all of us, the translations attempt to lure the reader into developing a "scientific" attitude toward man and his actions, a "scientific" understanding of the unconscious and how it conditions much of our behavior.

I became aware of this in the 1940s, when I became director of the University of Chicago's Orthogenic School, for disturbed children. The staff members I worked with were well read in Freud; they were convinced that they had made his ideas their own, and they tried to put their understanding of Freud into practice in their work with the children. The considerable theoretical understanding of unconscious processes which they had acquired from studying Freud remained exactly that: theoretical. It was of little use in helping children afflicted by severe psychiatric disorders; often it was even an impediment. It was a reasoned-out, emotionally distant understanding. What was needed was emotional closeness based on an immediate sympathetic comprehension of all aspects of the child's soul—of what afflicted it, and why. What was needed was what Freud occasionally spoke of explicitly but much more often implicitly: a spontaneous sympathy of our unconscious with that of others, a feeling response of our soul to theirs. By reading Freud in translation, the staff members had missed all this—one cannot be expected to gain an understanding of the soul if the soul is never mentioned.

The biggest shortcoming of the translations is that, through their use of abstractions, they make it easy for the reader to distance himself from what Freud sought to teach about the inner life of man and of the reader himself. Psychoanalysis becomes in English translation something that refers and applies to others as a system of intellectual constructs. Therefore, students of psychoanalysis are not led to take it personally—they are not moved to gain access to their own unconscious and everything else within them that is most human but is nevertheless unacceptable to them.

For nearly forty years, I have taught courses in psychoanalysis to American graduate students and residents in psychiatry. Again and again, I have been made to see how seriously the English translations impede students' efforts to gain a true understanding of Freud and of psychoanalysis. Although most of the bright and dedicated students whom it has been my pleasure to teach were eager to learn what psychoanalysis is all about, they were largely unable to do so. Almost invariably, I have found that psychoanalytic concepts had become for these students a way of looking only at others, from a safe distance—nothing that had any bearing on them. They observed other people through the spectacles of abstraction, tried to comprehend them by means of intellectual concepts, never turning their gaze inward to the soul or their own unconscious. This was true even of the students who were in analysis themselves—it made no appreciable difference. Psychoanalysis had helped some of them to be more at peace with themselves and to cope with life, had helped others to free themselves of troublesome neurotic symptoms, but their misconceptions about psychoanalysis remained. Psychoanalysis as these students perceived it was a purely intellectual system—a clever, exciting game—rather than the acquisition of insights into oneself and one's own behavior which were potentially deeply upsetting. It was always *someone else's* unconscious they analyzed, hardly ever their own. They did not give enough thought to the fact that Freud, in order to create psychoanalysis and understand the workings of the unconscious, had had to analyze his *own* dreams, understand his *own* slips of the tongue and the reasons *he* forgot things or made various other mistakes.

The best explanation for these students' failure to grasp the essence of Freud's thinking is the universal wish to remain unaware of one's own unconscious. Freud, who understood very well that this would be true for his readers, tried to speak to them as directly as possible. When he wrote about himself and his patients, he wrote in a manner designed to induce the reader to recognize that he was speaking about us all—about the reader as much as about himself, his patients, and others. Freud's choice of words and his direct style serve the purpose of making the reader apply psychoanalytic insights to himself, because only from his inner experience can he fully understand what Freud was writing about.

The errors in the translations of Freud become particularly misleading when they are compounded by the unavoidable distortions arising from the span of time that separates us from the era in which Freud formulated his ideas. In translation, Freud's ideas had to be transferred not only into a different language but into a different cultural environment—one in which most readers have only a nodding acquaintance with classical European literature. So most of Freud's allusions fall on deaf ears. Many of the expressions he used have been reduced to mere technical terms; the key words no longer have a multiplicity of special connotations, even though Freud chose them because they carried deep meaning and were vibrant with special humanistic resonances.

II

Language is all-important in Freud's work; it is the supreme instrument of his craft. His use of the German language was not only masterly but often poetic—he nearly always expressed himself with true eloquence. This is well known and widely recognized among those familiar with German writings. It has been remarked frequently that Freud's case histories read as well as the best novels written in his time. Many German writers recognized Freud as a great stylist: Thomas Mann, referring to one of Freud's books, wrote that "in structure and form it is related to all great German essay writing, of which it is a masterpiece." Hermann Hesse praised Freud because his work "convinces both through its very high human and very high literary qualities," and added that his language, while "completely intellectual, is beautifully concise and exact in its definitions." Albert Einstein said that he admired Freud particularly for his achievement as a writer, and that he did not know any other contemporary who could present his subject with such mastery of the German language.[1] Indeed, Freud modeled his style on the German classics—most of all on Goethe, whom he read closely as a student and who influenced him profoundly. (It was Goethe, incidentally, who introduced the term "sublimate"—*sublimieren*—into the German language in reference to human feelings that must be worked at, improved, and elevated.)

Because Freud attached so much importance to finding the *mot juste*, his translators' clumsy substitutions and inexact use of language are all the more damaging to his ideas. Deprived of the right word or the appropriate phrasing, Freud's thoughts become not merely coarse or oversimplified but seriously distorted. Slipshod translations deprive his words of some or most of the subtle sensory tones and allusions that he deliberately evoked to permit the reader to understand what he had in mind, and to respond not only on an intellectual level but also on an emotional one—not merely with the conscious mind but also with the unconscious mind. Only by comprehending his writings on both levels is it possible to grasp Freud's full meaning, in all its subtlety and richness, and this is crucial for a correct understanding of psychoanalysis.

Whenever Freud thought it possible, he tried to communicate his new ideas in the most common terms, words that his readers had used since childhood; his great achievement as a stylist was to imbue these words with nuances, meanings, and insights that had not been part of their everyday

[1] These and many more expressions of admiration for Freud's literary mastership can be found in Walter Schönau's analysis of Freud's style: *Sigmund Freuds Prosa*. Germanistische Abhandlungen 25, Stuttgart, Metzlerische Verlagsbuchhandlung, 1968.

use. When he could not communicate sufficiently by using readily available familiar terms, he would create new words from common ones, sometimes by combining two words, which is a standard practice in the German language. Only if common words, even when they were invested with new meanings or used in combination or juxtaposition, seemed inadequate to express what he intended to convey did he resort to the use of Greek or Latin—to terms such as the "Oedipus complex," which are derived from classical myths. Even then, he chose words he thought would be familiar to his readers and thus be invested with connotations important in communicating both his overt and his deeper meanings. He assumed that his readers would be cultivated people who had been schooled in the classics, as he had been. (In Freud's day, *Gymnasium*, or secondary school, students were required to study Greek and Latin.)

III

Among the Greek words that Freud used in very significant ways are "Eros" and "erotic"; from these words is derived the important concept of erotogenic zones, the term Freud created to name areas of the body particularly sensitive to erotic stimulation, such as the oral, anal, and genital zones. The concept first appeared in *Three Essays on the Theory of Sexuality* (1905). In a preface to the fourth edition, written in 1920, Freud stressed "how closely the enlarged concept of sexuality of psychoanalysis coincides with the Eros of divine Plato." For readers who, like Freud, were steeped in the classic tradition, words such as "Eros" and "erotic" called up Eros's charm and cunning and—perhaps more important —his deep love for Psyche, the soul, to whom Eros is wedded in everlasting love and devotion. For those familiar with this myth, it is impossible to think of Eros without being reminded at the same time of Psyche, and how she had at first been tricked into believing that Eros was disgusting, with the most tragic consequences. To view Eros or anything connected with him as grossly sexual or monstrous is an error that, according to the myth, can lead to catastrophe. (It would be equally erroneous to confuse Eros with Cupid: Cupid is an irresponsible, mischievous little boy; Eros is fully grown, at the height of the beauty and strength of young manhood.) In order for sexual love to be an experience of true erotic pleasure, it must be imbued with beauty (symbolized by Eros) and express the longings of the soul (symbolized by Psyche). These were some of the connotations that Freud had in mind when he used words like "Eros" and "erotic." Devoid of such connotations, which are closely related to their classical origin, these words not only lose much of the meaning he wished them to evoke but may even be invested with meanings opposite to those he intended.

This is true of the word "psychoanalysis" itself, which Freud coined. Those who use this now-familiar term are usually vaguely aware that it combines two words of Greek origin, but few are conscious of the fact that the two words refer to strongly contrasting phenomena. "Psyche" is the soul—a term full of the richest meaning, endowed with emotion, comprehensively human and unscientific. "Analysis" implies a taking apart, a scientific examination. English readers of Freud are further thrown off by the fact that in English the accent in "psychoanalysis" is on "analysis," thus emphasizing the part of the word whose connotations are scientific. With the German word *Psychoanalyse*, on the other hand, the accent is on the first syllable—on "psyche," the soul. By coining the term "psychoanalysis" to describe his work, Freud wished to emphasize that by isolating and examining the neglected and hidden aspects of our souls we can acquaint ourselves with those aspects and understand the roles they play in our lives. It was Freud's emphasis on the soul that made his analysis different from all others. What we think and feel about man's soul—our own soul—is all-important in Freud's view. Unfortunately, when we now use the word "psyche" in the compound word "psychoanalysis" or in other compound words, such as "psychology," we no longer react to the words with the feelings that Freud intended to evoke. This was not true for his contemporaries in Vienna; for them, "psyche" used in any combination never lost its real meaning.

The story of Psyche may have been particularly attractive to Freud because she had to enter the underworld and retrieve something there before she could attain her apotheosis. Freud, similarly, had to dare to enter the underworld—in his case, the underworld of the soul—to gain his illumination. He alluded to the story of Amor (or Eros) and Psyche in his essay "The Theme of the Three Caskets" (1913), in which he analyzed the unconscious motives that may explain the frequently evoked image of the always fateful choice among three: three caskets in *The Mer-*

chant of Venice, three daughters in *King Lear*, three goddesses in the judgment of Paris, and three sisters of whom Psyche was the most beautiful. Freud tried to show that two related topics underlie this motif: the wish to believe that we have a choice where we have none, and a symbolic expression of the three fateful roles that the female plays in the life of the male—as mother, as beloved, and, finally, as the symbolic mother (Mother Earth) to whom man returns when he dies. The tale of Amor and Psyche describes the deep attachment of a mother to her son—the relationship that Freud considered the most unambivalent in a man's life. It also depicts the extreme jealousy that a mother feels for the girl her son loves. As Apuleius tells it, Psyche's beauty was so great that she was more venerated than Venus, and that outraged Venus. "With parted lips," Venus "kissed her son long and fervently" to persuade him to destroy Psyche. But, despite his mother's efforts to seduce him into doing her bidding, Amor falls deeply in love with Psyche. This only increases Venus's jealousy, and she sets out to destroy Psyche by demanding tasks of her that she thinks will kill her, including that of bringing a casket filled with "a day's worth of beauty" up from the underworld. And, to make sure of Amor, Venus locks him up. In desperation, Amor turns for help to his father, Jupiter, who, remembering his own amorous experiences, accepts Psyche as his son's bride.

In some respects, the story of Amor and Psyche is a counterpart of that of Oedipus, but there are important differences. The Oedipus legend tells of a father's fear that his son will replace him; to avert this, the father tries to destroy his son. Psyche's story tells of a mother who is afraid

that a young girl will replace her in the affections of mankind and of her son, and who therefore tries to destroy the
girl. But, while the tale of Oedipus ends tragically, the tale
of Amor and Psyche has a happy ending, and this fact is
significant. A mother's love for her son and her jealous rage
against the girl he prefers to her can be openly acknowl-
edged. That the young girl surpasses the mature woman in
beauty, that a son turns away from his mother to embrace
his bride, that a bride has to suffer from the jealousy of her
lover's mother—all this, although extremely troublesome,
accords with normal human emotions, and is in line with the
natural conflict of the generations. That is why in the end
Jupiter and Venus accept the situation; Amor and Psyche
celebrate their wedding in the presence of all the gods;
Psyche is made immortal; and Venus makes peace with her.
But Oedipus, in killing his father and marrying his mother,
acts out in reality a common childhood fantasy that ought
to have remained just that. In doing so, Oedipus acts against
nature, which requires that a son marry a woman of his own
generation, and not his mother, and that he make his peace
with his father. Thus, his story results in tragedy for all
involved in the events.

Whether Freud was impressed by the parallels and differences of these two ancient myths we do not know, but
we do know how fascinated he was by Greek mythology:
he studied it assiduously, and he collected Greek, Roman,
and Egyptian statuary. He knew that Psyche was depicted
as young and beautiful, and as having the wings of a bird or
a butterfly. Birds and butterflies are symbols of the soul in
many cultures, and serve to emphasize its transcendental
nature. These symbols invested the word "psyche" with

connotations of beauty, fragility, and insubstantiality—ideas we still connect with the soul—and they suggest the great respect, care, and consideration with which Psyche had to be approached, because any other approach would violate, even destroy her. Respect, care, and consideration are attitudes that psychoanalysis, too, requires.

IV

The purpose of Freud's lifelong struggle was to help us understand ourselves, so that we would no longer be propelled, by forces unknown to us, to live lives of discontent, or perhaps outright misery, and to make others miserable, very much to our own detriment. In examining the content of the unconscious, Freud called into question some deeply cherished beliefs, such as the unlimited perfectibility of man and his inherent goodness; he made us aware of our ambivalences and of our ingrained narcissism, with its origins in infantile self-centeredness, and he showed us its destructive nature. In his life and work, Freud truly heeded the admonition inscribed on the temple of Apollo at Delphi—"Know thyself"—and he wanted to help us do the same. But to know oneself profoundly can be extremely upsetting. It implies the obligation to change oneself—an arduous and painful task. Many of the current misconceptions about Freud and psychoanalysis have arisen from the fear of self-knowledge—from the comforting view, abetted by the emotionally distancing language of the translations, that psychoanalysis is a method of analyzing selected aspects of the behavior of other people. Freud's insights threaten our narcissistic image of ourselves. How ironic that the work of a man who strove ardently for self-understanding should have led to so many defensive misconceptions about psychoanalysis!

By selectively accepting only some of Freud's ideas about the role of the sexual drives in man's makeup, and by misunderstanding his tragic belief that man's destructive tendencies spring from a dark side of the soul, and perverting this belief into a facile theory that the negative aspects of man's behavior are merely the consequence of his living in a bad society, many of Freud's followers have transformed psychoanalysis from a profound view of man's condition into something shallow. Freud was convinced that the creation of civilized society, despite all its shortcomings, was still man's noblest achievement. Only by seriously misinterpreting what Freud wrote in *Totem and Taboo* (1912–13) and *Civilization and Its Discontents* (1930) can one arrive at the comfortable assumption that psychoanalysis, instead of confronting us with the abyss within ourselves and forcing on us the incredibly difficult task of taming and controlling its chaos, would make life easy and pleasurable, and permit us, on the pretext of self-expression, to indulge our sexual desires without any restraints, risks, or price. All of Freud's work to uncover the unconscious was intended to give us some degree of rational control over it, so that when acting in line with its pressures was not appropriate, the releasing of these pressures could be postponed or neutralized, or—most desirable of all—the powers of the unconscious could be redirected through sublimation to serve higher and better purposes.

The difficulties that Freud experienced during his self-analysis and the difficulties that his patients had in summoning up the memories they had repressed made it obvious to him that the discovery of one's unconscious could never be easy. Some early experiences taught him that careful control over the patient's positive transference to the analyst and over the analyst's own feelings was absolutely necessary, in order to avoid undesirable consequences. He concluded that a special setting was required if the psychoanalytic work of self-discovery was to proceed safely and effectively. For the patient to safely open the caldron of the unconscious, setting free his emotions and undoing repressions—many of which had been quite useful in carrying on with the task of living in society—it was necessary to restrict the process to relatively short and well-circumscribed periods. Only then could one venture to unleash thoughts and feelings that, for one's own good and that of others, ordinarily had to be kept under control. Only then could one take a good look at what went on in one's unconscious without incurring the danger that this process would interfere with one's normal life outside the treatment room, and disrupt one's personal relations.

Freud's cautious approach has been disregarded in many quarters, and it has come to be popularly assumed that psychoanalysis advocates an unrestrained letting-go, not through talking in seclusion for a strictly limited period of time but through behaving without restraint all the time in all situations, regardless of the havoc this might play in one's own life and the lives of others. Because psychoanalysis has revealed the crippling consequences of too much repression, it has come to be assumed that it advocates the absence of all controls. Because psychoanalysis requires that "it should all come out"—though only for some fifty minutes a day, and under the guidance of a specially trained and trustworthy therapist, who will protect one from going too far or too fast in uncovering the unconscious—it has come to be assumed that psychoanalysis advocates "letting it all hang out," all over the place, all the time. "Know thyself" has become "Do whatever you please."

Freud repeatedly stressed that the enemies—the detractors—of psychoanalysis posed no danger to its development; his concern was with the naïve friends of his new science and with those who would use it to justify whatever their selfish desires led them to do and to inflict on others. He feared that psychoanalysis would be destroyed if it was widely accepted without being understood. After visiting the United States—where, in 1909, at Clark University, he received his first and only honorary degree for his achievements—Freud predicted that psychoanalysis was likely to suffer such a fate in this country. In 1930, he wrote,

> I often hear that psychoanalysis is very popular in the United States and that it doesn't meet there with the same obstinate resistance as it does in Europe. . . . It seems to me that the popularity of the name of psychoanalysis in America signifies neither a friendly attitude to its essence nor any extension and deepening of its understanding. . . . Most frequently one finds among American doctors and writers only a very inadequate familiarity with psychoanalysis, so

that they know only some names and slogans, which does not prevent them from certainty in making judgments.[1]

Like the father of American psychology, William James, Freud based his work mainly on introspection—his own and that of his patients. Introspection is what psychoanalysis is all about. Although Freud is often quoted today in introductory psychology texts—more often, in fact, than any other writer on psychology[2]—his writings have only superficially influenced the work of the academic psychologists who quote him. Psychological research and teaching in American universities are either behaviorally, cognitively, or physiologically oriented and concentrate almost exclusively on what can be measured or observed from the outside; introspection plays no part. American psychology has become all analysis—to the complete neglect of the psyche, or soul.

In the field of developmental psychology—which would hardly exist without Freud—most references to Freud's work are either refutations or trivializations of his ideas. Dr. Benjamin Spock, the most famous pediatrician of his day, applies many of Freud's insights into the minds of children in his book *Baby and Child Care*. In one of the two passages where he mentions Freud, Spock writes, "[The child's] previous intense attachments to his two parents will have served

[1] Introduction to an article in the *Medical Review of Reviews*, 36, 1930.
[2] In a recent tally, Freud topped the list with 318 citations. Next came Skinner with 140, and Piaget with 107. See N. S. Endler, J. P. Rushton, and H. L. Roediger, "Productivity and Scholarly Impact (citations) of British, Canadian, and U.S. Departments of Psychology 1975." *American Psychologist*, 1978, 33.

their main constructive purpose and will be progressively outgrown. (Freud called this shift the resolution of the Oedipus complex.)" It is as simple as that! Attachments serve purposes and are outgrown, without any conflict or residues. The Oedipus complex, Spock seems to think, disappears automatically with the passage of time—even though Freud showed how deeply the Oedipus complex shapes us all through life.

V

Freud coined the term "Oedipus complex" to describe the welter of ideas, emotions, and impulses, all largely or entirely unconscious, that center around the relations a child forms to his parents. It is impossible to understand why Freud chose this particular term—this metaphor—if one is not familiar with the important details of Oedipus's story. Unfortunately, most of the American graduate students whom I have tried to acquaint with psychoanalysis have had only the scantest familiarity with either the myth of Oedipus or Sophocles's play *Oedipus Rex.*

The story of Oedipus begins with the incredibly severe psychological and physical traumatization of a child by those who should be his prime protectors: his parents. The infant Oedipus—born of Laius and Jocasta, the King and Queen of Thebes, who have been warned by an oracle that their son is fated to murder his own father—is maimed (a spike thrust through his feet) and sent away to be killed. Spared from this early death, Oedipus is raised by the King and Queen of Corinth, and he grows up believing them to be his true parents. When, one day, someone suggests to him that they are not, Oedipus becomes so concerned that he consults the oracle at Delphi. The oracle tells Oedipus—just as his true parents have been told—that he will slay his father and marry his mother.

Shocked by this prophecy, Oedipus so strongly desires to protect those who he thinks are his parents that he flees Corinth, determined never to return. He begins wandering through Greece, where, at a crossroads, he meets, quarrels with, and murders a stranger: his father, Laius. Eventually, Oedipus arrives at Thebes, at a time when the city is ravaged by the Sphinx, who has settled on a nearby cliff, posing riddles to all who attempt to pass by and destroying anyone who cannot give the correct answer. Oedipus, homeless and caring little for his life, accepts the Sphinx's challenge. When he succeeds in solving the riddle she poses to him, he is rewarded by being made King of Thebes and he marries Jocasta. Many years later, a plague descends on the city as punishment for the unavenged murder of Laius. Oedipus is forced to try to find the murderer, and, when the truth is revealed, he blinds himself and Jocasta commits suicide.

The meaning of the term "Oedipus complex" is symbolic. Like all the metaphors Freud used in his writings, this term is valuable primarily for its suggestiveness and referential richness. It is a metaphor operating on many levels, since it alludes to other metaphors by its overt and covert references to the myth and the drama. Freud chose it to illumine and vivify a concept that defies more concise expression. If

we believe, as many of my students did, that the term "Oedipus complex" implies only that little boys want to kill the
man they *know* is their father and marry the woman they
know is their mother, then our understanding is based on an
extreme simplification of the myth. After all, Oedipus did
not know what he was doing when he killed Laius and
married Jocasta, and his greatest desire was to make it *impossible* for himself to harm those he thought were his parents.
What this term should suggest to us are the child's anxiety
and guilt for having patricidal and incestuous wishes, as well
as the consequences of acting on these wishes.

Oedipus's guilt and his discovery of the truth are the
central issues in Sophocles's play, and they are reflected in
the main features of the Oedipus complex. Freud found that
when we are no longer children we are unaware of the
negative feelings about the parent of the same sex and the
sexual feelings about both our parents that we had at an early
age, because we have deeply repressed many aspects of these
feelings. Second, although these complex and ambivalent
feelings about our parents are unknown to us as adults, we
continue to be unconsciously motivated by them and we
unconsciously feel guilty for them. These unconscious
desires and unconscious guilt feelings can have devastating
consequences. Finally, when the repressed hostility against
the parent of the same sex and the sexual longings for the
parent of the opposite sex at last become accessible to our
conscious recognition, then we can take actions to stop the
terrible consequences of these feelings.

In thinking about the Oedipus complex, we must keep
in mind what both the myth and Sophocles's play tell us:
that Oedipus acted as he did because his parents completely

rejected him as an infant, and that a child who was not utterly rejected by both his parents would never act as Oedipus did. Freud's ideas about the deep repression of Oedipal wishes and the severity of Oedipal guilt—so very important for understanding the conflict that shapes much of our personality—make no sense if our father has actually tried to kill us when we were infants; why would we feel guilty for wishing to get rid of such a villain? And the wish to love and to be loved exclusively and forever by our mother, as well as the guilt for wishing to possess her, makes no sense if our mother has actually turned against us when we were young. It is only our love for our parents and our conscious wish to protect them that leads us to repress our negative and sexual feelings directed toward them. These hidden feelings are what Freud referred to when he spoke of Oedipal guilt.

Oedipus, in fleeing Corinth, paid no attention to the admonitory temple inscription "Know thyself." The inscription implicitly warned that anyone who did not know himself would misunderstand the sayings of the oracle. Because Oedipus was unaware of his innermost feelings, he fulfilled the prophecy. Because he was unknowing of himself, he believed that he could murder the father who had raised him well, and marry the mother who loved him as a son. Oedipus acted out his metaphorical blindness—his blindness to what the oracle had meant, based on his lack of knowledge of himself—by depriving himself of his eyesight. In doing so, he may have been inspired by the example of Teiresias, the blind seer who reveals to Oedipus the truth about Laius's murder. We encounter in Teiresias the idea that having one's sight turned away from the external world and directed inward—toward the inner nature of things—

gives true knowledge and permits understanding of what is hidden and needs to be known.

The guiding principle of psychoanalysis is that knowing oneself requires knowing also one's unconscious and dealing with it, so that its unrecognized pressures will not lead one to act in a way detrimental to oneself and others. With this in mind, the self-knowledge required for a true understanding of the sayings of the oracle might be seen as extending to the normally unconscious aspects of ourselves. Freud's concept of the Oedipus complex thus contains the implied warning that we need to become aware of our unconscious. If we do, we will then be able to control it. When we then find ourselves at a crossroads, not knowing which way to turn and feeling blocked by some father figure, we will not strike out at him in uncontrolled anger and frustration. We will not, in moments of great stress, be pushed by our unconscious to act in ways that will destroy us, as Oedipus's actions destroyed him.

It is very much part of the Oedipus myth—and hence, by implication, of the Oedipus complex—that as long as the Oedipal deed and the unconscious Oedipal wishes, aggressions, and anxieties that led to the deed remain unknown, they continue to exert their destructive power; the pestilence that ravaged Thebes symbolizes this. When Oedipus learns the true cause of the pestilence, he cleanses himself, and the pestilence stops. This is a crucial part of the myth: as soon as the unknown is made known—as soon as the secret of the father's murder and the incest with the mother are brought to light, and the hero purges himself—the pernicious consequences of the Oedipal deeds disappear. The myth also warns that the longer one defends oneself against knowing these secrets, the greater is the damage to oneself and to others. The psychoanalytic construct of the Oedipus complex contains this implicit warning, too. Freud discovered, both in his self-analysis and in his work with his patients, that when one has the courage to face one's own unconscious patricidal and incestuous desires—which is tantamount to purging oneself of them—the evil consequences of these feelings subside. He found that becoming aware of our unconscious feelings—which makes them no longer unconscious but part of our conscious mind—is the best protection against an Oedipal catastrophe.

It is just possible that in developing his theory of the Oedipus complex Freud subconsciously responded to his familiarity with the myth of Oedipus and with Sophocles's tragedy because both warn of the utterly destructive consequences of acting *without knowing* what one is doing. Freud's discoveries permit us to understand also the deeper meaning of the story of the Sphinx, which probably had its origin in the unconscious insights of the myth's inventors. The Oedipus legend juxtaposes the radically opposite outcomes of our actions when we are driven by unconscious pressures, as Oedipus was when he killed Laius, and when we are free of such pressures, as Oedipus was in his encounter with the Sphinx. The Sphinx, not being a father figure, did not arouse psychological ambivalences and difficulties in Oedipus, so that, when meeting the Sphinx, he was in full possession of all his rational powers and thus was easily able to solve the Sphinx's riddle. Freud showed how this applies to all of us: when we are able to confront dark forces with the powers of our rational mind, unencumbered by unconscious pressures, then rationality wins out; and when rationality dominates our actions, we can overcome the destructive powers and free ourselves of their ability to harm us.

The Sphinx, who posed riddles and devoured those who could not solve them, was herself a riddle, since she was part woman and part destructive animal. The upper part of her body was that of a woman with prominent breasts; the lower part, the part in which her sexual organs are located, was that of a lion with terrible claws. She is at once a symbol of the good, nurturing mother and of the bad, destructive mother. She symbolizes the child's fear that, because he wishes to devour his mother so that she will be all his, never able to leave him (an idea that has its origins in the fact that the child eats off his mother, tries to swallow part of her body as he nurses), she will retaliate by devouring him.

Because we are told that the Sphinx posed all sorts of riddles, we must assume that the one she asked Oedipus was designed specifically for him. The riddle went as follows: "In the morning it goes on four feet, at noon on two, and in the evening on three," and "Just when it walks on most feet, its speed and strength are at their lowest ebb." The correct answer, which Oedipus supplied, was "man"—for in the "morning" of his life (infancy) he crawls about on all fours, at "noon" (the prime of life) he walks on two feet, and in the "evening" (old age) he requires the assistance of a "third foot," that is, a cane or walking stick; and, of course, it is in infancy, when he has the "most feet," that he also has the least strength and speed of movement. But, as Thomas De Quincey has pointed out, the subject of the riddle, and also its solution, is not just man in general but Oedipus in particular: nobody is as weak at birth as the abandoned infant with its feet pinned together, and nobody needs more assistance in old age than Oedipus did in his years of blindness. Certainly Oedipus, owing to the lasting effects of his early trauma, must have been more concerned with the problems posed by walking than most people are, and more likely to think of walking and what it means at various ages; as an infant, crawling on all fours, he must have been more keenly aware than an ordinary child of his inability to walk on two feet. What the story of the Sphinx seems to emphasize is that the answer to the riddle of life is not just man, but each person himself. Thus, the myth tells us again that we must know ourselves in order to free ourselves from destructive powers.

In Freud's system, Oedipal desires and castration anxiety are closely connected: castration anxiety contributes to the abandonment of Oedipal strivings and leads to the development of the controlling institutions of the mind and morality. Today we think that the child's love for his parents also has a great deal to do with these developments. Shakespeare recognized this when, in Sonnet CLI, he wrote, "Yet who knows not conscience is born of love?" Freud believed it was the father's fear of being replaced, of being overcome by his son, that accounted for the practice of circumcision—a symbolic castration—in primitive societies. Since the time Freud expressed these ideas doubts have arisen about his views on the meaning of circumcision,[1] but it is certain that he recognized the role parental attitudes play in the formation and the resolution of the Oedipus complex. The importance of parental attitudes is clearly indicated in the myth.

[1] See, among other writings, my own book *Symbolic Wounds*.

Had Oedipus's parents not believed in the oracle's prediction, they would not have attempted to murder their son. It was common knowledge at the time that the sayings of the Pythia were ambiguous and difficult to interpret correctly. For Laius and Jocasta to accept this prophecy uncritically, they must have been convinced that their interpretation of the oracle was correct, just as Oedipus was convinced that his interpretation was correct and that the oracle was referring to his foster parents. What convinced Oedipus were the Oedipal feelings he had developed toward those who had raised him from infancy; what convinced his parents were their feelings toward their child, feelings that are as much a part of the Oedipus complex as are those of the child.

Laius's interpretation of the oracle's saying seemed plausible to him because he feared that his son would replace him: initially, in the affections of his wife, and, later, in his role in society. While the first of these fears is often—albeit not always—unwarranted, the second is not, since in the normal course of events the son replaces the father in society as the father grows old and the son achieves manhood. Jocasta must have feared that she might love her son more than she loved her husband; otherwise, she would have tried to persuade Laius that he had misunderstood the meaning of the prophecy and that no son of theirs would do what had been predicted. If she had not had such fears, she would never have agreed to have Oedipus sent away to die but would have made some effort to rescue him. It was because she did not—because she participated in the plot to kill her son—that Jocasta later killed herself. Her suicide had nothing to do with guilt for her incest with Oedipus, as many of my students believed it did; Sophocles makes this clear.

The Oedipus legend thus foreshadows the psychoanalytic finding that the Oedipal wishes and anxieties of the child have their counterparts in the feelings of the parents toward the child. These feelings are the parents' attraction to the child of the opposite sex and their ambivalence about (or even resentment of) the child of the same sex, who they fear will replace them. If parents permit themselves to be dominated by these feelings, then the kind of tragedy results that both the myth and Sophocles's play tell about.

There is still much to be learned about Freud's life, work, and thoughts, since many important records are still locked up in the Freud Archives in the Library of Congress and will not become available until the year 2000. I doubt, though, that even when these archives are opened we will attain certainty about all the conscious and subconscious thoughts that went into Freud's formation of the concept of the Oedipus complex; it was too difficult to develop and took too long to arrive at. This is suggested by the fact that more than ten years elapsed between Freud's first mention of Sophocles's *Oedipus* in connection with what he was discovering about children's unconscious feelings toward their parents (this was in a letter to his friend Wilhelm Fliess, written at the time of Freud's self-analysis) and his actual naming of the Oedipus complex in a publication.

As early as 1900 Freud wrote of the similarities between psychoanalysis and *Oedipus Rex*: "The action of the play consists in nothing other than the process of revealing, step by step, with mounting excitement and cunning delays— comparable to the work of psychoanalysis—that Oedipus himself is not only the murderer of Laius but also the son of the murdered man and of Jocasta." In contemplating Sophocles's *Oedipus* as Freud did, one realizes that the entire play is essentially Oedipus's struggle to get at the hidden truth. It is a battle for knowledge in which Oedipus has to overcome tremendous inner resistance against recognizing the truth about himself, because he fears so much what he might discover. Anyone who is familiar with the tragedy, as Freud expected his readers to be, cannot help being impressed that Sophocles does not present the Oedipal deed; even the Oedipal wishes are mentioned only briefly, in Jocasta's remark: "Nor need this mother-marrying frighten you; many a man has dreamt as much." In a way, Sophocles's play seems to imply that (the wish) to do away with the father and (the wish) to marry the mother is fate, just as the myth says it is, and that is that. What forms the essence of our humanity—and of the play—is not our being victims of fate, but our struggle to discover the truth about ourselves. Jocasta, who clearly states that she does not wish to discover the truth, cannot face it when it is revealed, and she perishes. Oedipus, who does face the truth, despite the immense dangers to himself of which he is at least dimly aware, survives. Oedipus suffers much, but at the end, at Colonus, he not only finds peace, but is called to the god and becomes transfigured.

What is most significant about Oedipus, the Oedipal situation, and the Oedipus complex is not only the tragic fate that we all are projected into deep conflicts by our infantile desires, but also the need to resolve these conflicts through the difficult struggle for, and the achievement of, self-discovery. This is why, as Freud always insisted, the Oedipus complex is central to psychoanalysis.

VI

Accepting the idea of the Oedipus complex without understanding the myth and the play from which it got its name is one way of accepting psychoanalysis without trying to get at its deeper meaning—just what Freud predicted would happen in the United States. Since Freud's translators envisaged a large English and American readership, and since American readers, at least, tend to be unfamiliar with most of the story of Oedipus and Freud's other classical references, it would have been helpful if the translators had made some attempt to explain the meaning of Freud's allusions to classical literature. It can be argued that translators ought to concern themselves with rendering only what the author wrote, as closely as the difference in languages permits. But to deal accurately with a subject such as psychoanalysis, and with language so carefully chosen for nuances as Freud's was, translators need to be very sensitive not only to what is written but also to what is implied. Their task very definitely includes an obligation to try to transmit not just the words forming a sentence but also the meanings to which these words allude. The translators must be responsive to the author's efforts to speak also to the reader's subconscious, to arouse an emotional response as well as an intellectual one. In short, they must also translate the author's attempts to convey covert meanings.

I do not doubt that Freud's English translators wanted to present his writings to their audience as accurately as possible—in terms of the frame of reference within which they wished him to be understood. When Freud appears to be either more abstruse or more dogmatic in English translation than in the original German, to speak about abstract concepts rather than about the reader himself, and about man's mind rather than about his soul, the probable explanation isn't mischievousness or carelessness on the translators' part but a deliberate wish to perceive Freud strictly within the framework of medicine, and, possibly, an unconscious tendency to distance themselves from the emotional impact of what Freud tried to convey.

The English translations cleave to an early stage of Freud's thought, in which he inclined toward science and medicine, and disregard the more mature Freud, whose orientation was humanistic, and who was concerned mostly with broadly conceived cultural and human problems and with matters of the soul. Freud himself stated that he considered the cultural and human significance of psychoanalysis more important than its medical significance.

In summing up, in the thirty-fourth of the *New Introductory Lectures on Psychoanalysis* (1933), what he viewed as the main merits of psychoanalysis, Freud, while remarking on its therapeutic successes, did not hide its limitations in this respect; in fact, he admitted that he was never really enthusiastic about psychoanalysis as therapy. While psychoanalysis is beyond doubt the most valuable method of psychotherapy, that is only to be expected, since it is the most difficult, demanding, and time-consuming method. Freud recommended psychoanalysis to our interest "not as therapy but rather because of what it reveals to us about what concerns man most closely: his own essence; and because of the connections it uncovers between the widest variety of his actions." His greatest hope was that with the spreading of psychoanalytic knowledge, and the insights gained through it, the rearing of children would be reformed. Freud considered this "perhaps the most important of all activities of analysis," because it could free the largest number of people —not merely the few who underwent analysis personally— from unnecessary repressions, unrealistic anxieties, and destructive hatreds. By vastly reducing the inner conflicts from which we suffered, psychoanalysis could help us to act more rationally—could help us, in short, to become more human. "Psychoanalysis is not a medical specialty," Freud said in his "Postscript to 'The Question of Lay Analysis' " (1927). "I do not see how one can resist recognizing this. Psychoanalysis is a part of psychology. It is not medical psychology in the traditional sense, nor the psychology of pathological processes. It is psychology proper; certainly not all of psychology, but its substratum, possibly its very foundation." He went on to warn that one should not permit oneself to be led astray by its application for medical purposes; he compared psychoanalysis to electricity, which has its medical uses in the form of x-ray techniques, pointing out that this does not make electricity become part of medicine rather than part of physics.

Despite this clear-cut assertion, psychoanalysis was perceived in the United States as a practice that ought to be the sole prerogative of physicians, instead of being accepted for what it is in the deepest and most important sense: a call to greater humanity, and a way to achieve it. So adamant were the American analysts that psychoanalysis must be restricted to physicians that in 1926 the New York State Legislature passed a bill declaring illegal any analysis not conducted by a physician. Not satisfied with this, the Americans continued their battle within the International Psycho-Analytical Association, and threatened to break away from the international psychoanalytic movement unless their view was accepted. A struggle over this issue led to severe dissensions within the International Psycho-Analytical Association, which lasted from 1926 until 1932, when Ernest Jones, the chairman of a committee set up by the association to deal with the problem, worked out a compromise, according to which each of the national societies forming the international association would thereafter have the right to determine the qualifications needed for membership. As a result, the American analysts decided—very much against Freud's strong convictions—that, as a general principle, in the United States only physicians could become analysts.

The consequences of this action were to be far-reaching, though nobody suspected as much at the time. When Freud reluctantly acquiesced in the decision of the American analysts, the center of psychoanalysis was in Europe, with the Viennese group around Freud clearly dominant. All seven members of the "Committee" that directed the psychoanalytic movement lived in Europe: Freud and Otto Rank in Vienna; Karl Abraham, Max Eitingon, and Hanns Sachs in Berlin; Sandor Ferenczi in Budapest; and Ernest Jones in London. No one imagined that the small and relatively insignificant group of analysts in the United States could have the slightest influence on the overall development of psychoanalysis, since all theoretical and practical advances originated in the European centers, mainly with Freud himself, his daughter Anna, and the other members of the "Committee." With the advent of Hitler, however, everything suddenly changed. Psychoanalysis disappeared on the Continent, and after the war the American psychoanalysts were the largest and most influential group, dominating the entire field. It is at the very least doubtful that if Freud had foreseen this situation he would have agreed that psychoanalysis in the United States might become a medical specialty, since whenever he had felt strongly about an issue he risked splits in the psychoanalytic movement to assure its continuation in his spirit.

The strength of Freud's conviction that psychoanalysis should not exist solely within a medical framework can be gauged from a 1928 letter to his friend Oskar Pfister. Referring to two of his recent books, *The Question of Lay Analysis* (1926), in which he had argued that psychoanalytically trained laymen should be permitted to treat patients, and *The Future of an Illusion* (1927), which dealt with the nature of religious ideas, he wrote, "I do not know whether you have guessed the hidden link between 'Lay Analysis' and 'Illusion.' In the former I want to protect analysis from physicians, and in the latter from priests. I want to entrust it to a profession that doesn't yet exist, a profession of secular ministers of souls, who don't have to be physicians and must not be priests."[1] Psychoanalysis was to be neither a medical discipline nor a creed. Psychoanalysts were not to think or function as the healers of bodies do, nor were they to be

---

[1] What I have translated as "ministers of souls" is, in the original, *Seelsorger*, a term normally applied to priests and ministers. Freud used it in a broader sense, combining *Seele*, which means "soul," and *Sorger*, which means "somebody who ministers to needs."

purveyors of an esoteric or revealed truth. (Incidentally, in its original American edition, published in 1927, the title of *The Question of Lay Analysis—Die Frage der Laienanalyse—* was mistranslated as *The Problem of Lay-Analyses.* By the time the book was republished under its correct title, in 1947, the damage was done.)

During the last months of Freud's life, when psychoanalysis had almost ceased to exist on the continent of Europe, it was widely rumored that he had changed his mind and was of the opinion that the practice of psychoanalysis should be confined to physicians. In answer to an inquiry on this matter, he wrote (in English): "I cannot imagine how that silly rumor of my having changed my views about the problem of Lay-Analysis may have originated. The fact is, I have never repudiated these views and I insist on them even more intensely than before, in the face of the obvious American tendency to turn psychoanalysis into a mere housemaid of Psychiatry."

To characterize the function of the analyst—someone who could greatly facilitate the emergence of a new personality, making the process of the change a safe one—Freud often used the simile of the midwife. As the midwife neither creates the child nor decides what he will be but only helps the mother to give birth to him safely, so the psychoanalyst can neither bring the new personality into being nor determine what it ought to be; only the person who is analyzing himself can make himself over. Others have also used the image of the midwife to explain the work of psychoanalysis. The poet H. D. (Hilda Doolittle), speaking of her experience with Freud during her analysis, said, "He is midwife to the soul."

VII

In the Vienna of Freud's time, psychology was not a natural science but a branch of philosophy; it was mainly speculative and descriptive, and was essentially humanistic in content. Not until the Second World War did psychology in Vienna move out of this frame of reference, and even then it did so only slowly and tentatively, as psychologists began to mimic students of the natural sciences in their methods and their thinking.

How Freud conceived of psychology can be seen from the way he spoke about it in *The Question of Lay Analysis:* "In psychology we can describe only with the help of comparisons. This is nothing special, it is the same elsewhere. But we are forced to change these comparisons over and over again, for none of them can serve us for any length of time." There are several reasons for Freud's frequent use of metaphors in explaining the nature of psychoanalysis. One is that psychoanalysis, though it is confronted with hard, objective facts, does not deal with them as such but devotes itself to the imaginative interpretation and explanation of hidden causes, which can only be inferred. The metaphors that Freud used were intended to bridge the rift that exists between the hard facts to which psychoanalysis refers and the imaginative manner in which it explains them. A second reason is even more closely related to the nature of psychoanalysis. Because of repression, or the influence of censorship, the unconscious reveals itself in symbols or metaphors, and psychoanalysis, in its concern with the unconscious, tries to speak about it in its own metaphoric language. Finally, metaphors are more likely than a purely intellectual statement to touch a human chord and arouse our emotions, and thus give us a feeling for what is meant. A true comprehension of psychoanalysis requires not only an intellectual realization but a simultaneous emotional response; neither alone will do. A well-chosen metaphor will permit both.

Because poets speak in metaphors about the contents of their unconscious, Freud insisted that they, and other great artists, knew all along what he had to discover through laborious work. Throughout his psychoanalytic writings, Freud discussed works of art and literature in an attempt to appeal to our intuitions, to engage both our unconscious and our conscious understanding. He often quoted Goethe, Shakespeare, and other poets, as well as such writers as Dostoevsky, Nietzsche, and Arthur Schnitzler, and he maintained that they knew everything that needs to be known about the unconscious. All he claimed for himself was that he had organized this knowledge and made it available as a means of understanding the unconscious not only intuitively but also explicitly. Freud rarely quoted natural scientists, not to mention physicians; the only exceptions were his fellow psychoanalysts who were also physicians, and whom he had taught psychoanalysis in the first place.

Freud relished anecdotes and jokes, particularly Jewish jokes, because they were so pregnant with unconscious meanings. Like metaphors, jokes suggest rather than announce their meaning, and they invite the initiated to speculate about their unconscious origin. Freud devoted one of his major works to showing how cleverly, concisely, and amusingly jokes allow us deep insights into man's unconscious, and he used jokes for this purpose elsewhere in his writings. (Many of the Jewish jokes that were very popular with the Viennese intelligentsia in Freud's day asserted their cleverness while at the same time making fun of it, thus blunting the effect of their claim to superiority. The anti-Semitism that was rampant in Vienna aroused strong feelings among the Jewish population, feelings it may have been unwise to show openly, and Jewish jokes often permitted the ventilation of these feelings; they were often metaphors for the true feelings of Viennese Jews.)

For these and many parallel reasons, it is important, if we wish to understand Freud, to pay close attention to his use of metaphors, whether or not he makes it obvious that he is speaking metaphorically; it is equally important that we not take his metaphors as factual statements.

Of all the metaphors that Freud used, probably none had more far-reaching consequences than the metaphor of mental illness, and—derived from it—the metaphor of psychoanalysis as the treatment and cure of mental illness. Freud evoked the image of illness and its treatment to enable us to comprehend how certain disturbances influence the psyche, what causes them, and how they may be dealt with. If this metaphor is not recognized as such but, rather, taken as referring to objective facts, we forfeit a real understanding of the unconscious and its workings. In this metaphor, the body stands for the soul. If the metaphor is interpreted literally, as it has been in the United States, our psyche, or soul—for Freud the terms were interchangeable—seems to become something tangible. It acquires something akin to a physical existence, like a bodily organ; hence its treatment becomes part of medical science.

In the United States, of course, "the cure of mental illness" has been seen as the main task of psychoanalysis, just as the curing of bodily illness is that of medicine. It is expected that anyone undergoing psychoanalysis will achieve tangible results—the kind of results the physician achieves for the body—rather than a deeper understanding of himself and greater control of his life. In 1949 one of America's foremost psychologists declared at a meeting of the American Psychological Association that, of all the features of Freudian theory, the mechanisms of adjustment had become the most widely accepted in the United States. This remarkable statement reveals the nature of American acceptance of psychoanalysis, particularly since Freud cared little about "adjustment" and did not consider it valuable. What is true, and what this American spokesman for psychoanalysis should have said, is that the concept of adjustment was injected into the Freudian system because it was of primary importance in the American psychoanalysts' scheme of values, and that this alteration explains the widespread acceptance of psychoanalysis in America. If American psychoanalysts had shared Freud's concern for the soul, and his disregard for adaptation or adjustment to the requirements of society, then the history of psychoanalysis in the United States would be entirely different, since psychoanalysis would have had to transcend the narrow confines of medicine. But, of course, if this had happened, psychoanalysis might not have been successful in the United States.

In the German culture within which Freud lived, and which permeated his work, there existed and still exists a definite and important division between two approaches to knowledge. Both disciplines are called *Wissenschaften* (sciences), and they are accepted as equally legitimate in their appropriate fields, although their methods have hardly anything in common. These two are the *Naturwissenschaften* (natural sciences) and, opposed to them in content and in methods, the *Geisteswissenschaften*. The term *Geisteswissenschaften* defies translation into English; its literal meaning is "sciences of the spirit," and the concept is one that is deeply rooted in German idealist philosophy. These disciplines represent entirely different approaches to an understanding of the world. Renan, trying to translate them into French, suggested that they divided all knowledge into *la science de l'humanité* and *la science de la nature*. In such a division of knowledge, a hermeneutic-spiritual knowing and a positivistic-pragmatic knowing are opposed to each other. In much of the German world, and particularly in Vienna before and during Freud's life, psychology clearly fell into the realm of the first; in much of the English-speaking world, on the other hand, psychology clearly belonged to the *Naturwissenschaften*.

The influential German philosopher Wilhelm Windelband, Freud's contemporary, elaborated on the fundamental differences between these two approaches to knowledge. He classified the natural sciences as nomothetic, because they search for and are based on general laws, and in many of them mathematics plays an important role. The *Geisteswissenschaften* he called idiographic, because they seek to understand the objects of their study not as instances of universal laws but as singular events; their method is that of history, since they are concerned with human history and with individual ideas and values. Nomothetic sciences require verification through replication by experiment; their findings ought to permit mathematical and statistical analysis and, most important, ought to permit exact predictions. Idiographic sciences deal with events that never recur in the same form—that can be neither replicated nor predicted.

Psychoanalysis is concerned with the discovery of events in the past life of the individual and with their consequences for him, and neither the events nor the consequences can ever be exactly the same for two persons. Freud frequently compared psychoanalysis with archeology: the work of psychoanalysis consists in unearthing the deeply buried remnants of the past and combining them with other fragments that are more accessible; once all the pieces have been put together, it becomes possible to speculate about the origin and the nature of the individual psyche.

While Freud's vocation was psychoanalysis, his avocation was archeology. He read widely in both archeology and history, and little in the natural sciences. As I mentioned earlier, Freud avidly collected ancient Greek, Roman, and Egyptian antiques; he bought them even when the expense was burdensome. His treatment room and the desk at which he did all his writing were crowded with these antiques. During treatment he would sometimes use one of them to make a point, handing it to his patient to help him better understand a particular idea about the unconscious. These antiques were so important to Freud that he refused to leave Nazi-occupied Vienna, where his life was in danger, until he was assured that his collection could leave with him.

It is clear that Freud was deeply interested in prehistory: the prehistory of the modern world, which he sought to discover in ancient Egypt, Greece, and Rome; the prehistory of individual man, for which he searched in the childhood of the individual and in the individual's unconscious; the prehistory of the human race, which he sought to understand through the customs of primitive man; the prehistory of culture, for which he searched in totems and taboos, and in the role of Moses in the creation of monotheism. There can be little doubt that when he spoke of his *Wissenschaft*, psychoanalysis, Freud meant the study of the sources of humanity in all its various forms.

Psychoanalysis is plainly an idiographic science, utilizing unique historical occurrences to provide a view of man's development and behavior. Whether Freud analyzes his dreams, which are unique to him, or establishes the past history of patients, or discusses what constitutes the essence of a work of art and how it relates to the life and personality of the artist, or analyzes the origin of religion or rituals, the psychology of masses, or the basis of society or of monotheism, he is working within the framework of the *Geisteswissenschaften*, applying the methods appropriate to an idiographic science.

When the English-speaking reader is confronted with the word "science," however, he thinks of the natural sciences; and when he is confronted with the word "psychology" he is likely to think of it as a discipline that tries to be an exact science; that is, a science based on controlled experiments that can be replicated and studied statistically. If the conviction that psychoanalysis belongs to the field of medicine is added to this notion (wasn't Freud a physician who treated patients, and isn't the practice of psychoanalysis restricted to physicians?), it seems logical to interpret what

Freud wrote as part of a natural science, and to translate his writings accordingly.

In such a frame of mind, a translator of Freud will try to use precise terms, and make things clear and definite, however much treatises centering on the unconscious in all its manifestations may defy such efforts. If the translator is confronted with newly created terms that as yet have no English equivalent, he may translate them by creating new terms of his own, which permit clear definitions rather than evoke vague and emotionally loaded connotations, for he may believe Freud to have thought of or wished for such precision when he created his new terms. A translation prepared in this manner will then add to the impression that Freud's system is one of the natural sciences.

Such methods of translation are reinforced by the fact that English scientific writing requires a degree of clarity and definiteness that German writing does not. A type of expression that in English would be scorned as muddleheaded and confused is quite acceptable in German. While English authors, particularly in scientific writings, shun ambiguities, German writing is full of them. Psychoanalytic writing, which is concerned to such a large degree with the unconscious—itself full of ambiguities and contradictions—will in German try to do them justice, while good English style requires that such ambiguities be avoided. In theory, many topics with which Freud dealt permit both a hermeneutic-spiritual and a positivistic-pragmatic approach. When this is so, the English translators nearly always opt for the latter, positivism being the most important English philosophical tradition.

This is not to say that those who wish to see Freud as

a natural scientist, and psychoanalysis as a medical specialty, won't find some justification for their views in certain things he said. Freud was not a psychoanalyst all his life; he came to psychoanalysis in his forties. His pre-psychoanalytic work was in physiology and medicine. While studying physiology at the University of Vienna, Freud was much impressed by the scientific rigor that his mentors demonstrated and also demanded of others; he therefore made their methods and values his own. He continued to adhere to these for a time after he decided to become a physician in private practice, specializing in neurology. His attitudes changed only gradually.

Freud spoke in some detail about his desire at one time to devote his life to physiological research, in which he had been quite successful. He said he gave it up only for economic reasons. Both his character and his life history suggest, however, that economics cannot have been the full explanation; it may instead have been a convenient rationalization, which the claim that one does things for economic rewards often is. Freud wrote, too, about his failure to be recognized as the discoverer of the medicinal uses of cocaine. Yet he deprived himself of the credit for this great discovery when at a crucial moment in his research he left Vienna to visit his fiancée, whom he had managed quite well not to visit on other occasions. His actions in this instance make it seem that he unconsciously wished to give up his research career.

Freud was a very complex person, a man whose own inner conflicts prompted his self-analysis—the process through which he discovered psychoanalysis. It was this, his self-analysis, that was Freud's great transformation. His ideas underwent far-reaching evolutions in this process, and he therefore said different things about psychoanalysis at different times. But the various statements Freud made about the depth of his commitment to the natural sciences and their methods—statements he certainly believed at the time he made them—become open to question when one considers his humanism and his application of idiographic principles to the phenomena he tried to bring into his own and our understanding.

Much has been written about the significant role that Freud's intimate friendship with Wilhelm Fliess played in Freud's self-analysis. Fliess, a nose and throat specialist, was, like Freud, deeply interested in the profound importance of sexuality in man's life. Fliess was convinced that periodicity determines all biological processes, including birth, illness, and death. To prove this, he applied the most abstract discipline—mathematics—to the study of biology, making his mathematical speculations the basis for understanding all physiological processes. Freud tried to follow his friend's reasonings, but could never bring himself to do so fully. During his self-analysis, Freud was veering ever further away from the exact sciences. In one of his letters to Fliess, he wrote, "When there are two people, one of whom can say what life is, the other (almost) what the soul is, it is only right that they should see each other and talk together often." In this way, Freud distinguished between his own work, the study of the soul, and Fliess's work in the natural sciences.

As his self-analysis proceeded, Freud increasingly distanced himself from the natural sciences and from Fliess; in the end, he broke with Fliess completely. Nobody actually replaced Fliess as Freud's confidant and most intimate friend, but shortly after the break with Fliess, Freud began to correspond regularly and frequently with C. G. Jung. Like Fliess, Jung was a physician, but he was also a psychoanalyst and, as his later work shows, he was fascinated by myths and prehistory. These topics occupied Freud's mind a great deal, too, of course, and although his attitude toward and interest in religion were very different from Jung's, they both studied religion from a psychological point of view. Freud's shift from Fliess to Jung might be seen as a step in his inner development away from biology and toward the study of the soul.

Another example of how Freud moved away from the idea that psychoanalysis could be an exact science, permitting replication and predictions characteristic of the hard sciences, can be found in the evolution of his views on dream symbolism. In 1913, he wrote, in the paper "The Interest of Psychoanalysis," that psychoanalysts were "able to some extent to translate the content of dreams independently of the dreamer's associations." That is, Freud believed then that his "science" enabled him to say with some certainty what the appearance of a symbol in the dream of any patient meant. In 1925, in the paper "Some Additional Notes on Dream-Interpretation as a Whole," he wrote: "Dream interpretation . . . without reference to the dreamer's associations would . . . remain a piece of unscientific virtuosity of the most doubtful value." He had decided that to different persons the same symbol could have entirely different implications—that only a study of the individual's unique associations to a symbol permitted understanding of what it signified. He had become convinced that each psychological event had its own unique history, existed within a unique context, and could be understood only in that context.

Later, Freud realized even more clearly that the natural sciences had been a detour from what he really wanted to do with his life. In *The Question of Lay Analysis,* he wrote, "After forty-one years of medical activities, my self-knowledge tells me that I have not been a physician in the proper sense. I became a physician through being compelled to deviate from my original intention; and the triumph of my life lies in my having, after a great detour, found my way back to my original direction." Freud explained what this original direction was in his "Postscript to 'An Autobiographical Study' " (1935):

> After a lifelong detour over the natural sciences, medicine, and psychotherapy, my interests returned to those cultural problems which had once captivated the youth who had barely awakened to deeper thought. These interests had centered on "the events of the history of man, the mutual influences between man's nature, the development of culture, and those residues of prehistoric events of which religion is the foremost representation . . . studies which originate in psychoanalysis but go way beyond it."

Even before Freud stated so explicitly that it was not the natural sciences or medicine that stood at the center of his interests, an Englishman who considered himself a hard-nosed scientist recognized that Freud's primary commitment was to the humanities. Wilfred Trotter, whom Freud had extensively quoted in his book *Group Psychology and the*

Analysis of the Ego (1921), wrote, "However much one may be impressed by the greatness of the edifice which Freud has built up and by the soundness of his architecture, one can scarcely fail, on coming into it from the bracing atmosphere of the biological sciences, to be oppressed by the odour of humanity with which it is pervaded."

The issue that concerns me here is not whether or in what measure Freud saw himself at certain moments in his life as a natural scientist, and psychoanalysis as a natural science—for sometimes he did. My point is to question whether his English translators and, consequently, American students of psychoanalysis were not and are not led astray by Freud's statements along these lines to misconceive much else that he wrote, in which he clearly wanted us to accept psychoanalysis as a humanistic undertaking.

VIII

Most of Freud's writings were published in English during his lifetime, and all existing translations of his work into English were authorized either by Freud himself or by his estate. Since Freud read and wrote English fluently, it is hard to understand how he could have permitted translations that are faulty in both word and spirit, and that seriously impede readers' efforts to gain a true understanding of his work.

I first read Freud systematically in English translation in

the late 1940s, when some of my friends and colleagues at the University of Chicago became involved in preparing the Encyclopaedia Britannica publication *Great Books of the Western World*, the fifty-fourth and final volume of which was to be devoted entirely to Freud's writings. When consulted about which of his works should be included in this volume, I suggested that new translations were needed that would be more faithful both to what Freud actually wrote and to what he tried to convey. My arguments—based not only on my reading of Freud in English but also on what I had learned about the inability of my students and the staff of the Orthogenic School to comprehend Freud in translation—must have been fairly convincing. For a while, the editors considered commissioning new translations of the works selected. But in the end, time was too short, the expense too great, and there was small likelihood that Freud's heirs would give their permission.

A few years later, I was approached by one of the directors of a large foundation and offered the opportunity of preparing a new, annotated translation of Freud's writings. I was not inclined to accept this challenging offer because the task would have consumed the rest of my life, because I doubted the adequacy of my skills, and because I was deeply involved in the work of the Orthogenic School. There was also the familiar problem of whether the holders of the publishing rights would permit the publication of a new translation, particularly since an authorized edition of Freud's complete writings was already in preparation.

The twenty-four-volume *Standard Edition of the Complete Psychological Works of Sigmund Freud* was published in London by the Hogarth Press, and appeared between 1953 and 1974. The general editor of the series, James Strachey, had undergone analysis with Freud in Vienna after the First World War and had translated several of his works into English during Freud's lifetime. For the *Standard Edition*, Strachey either revised existing translations or, in some cases, provided completely new translations of his own. All the translations had the approval of Anna Freud. Because the translations in the *Standard Edition* are for the most part an improvement on those in the earlier editions—although many, many shortcomings remain—all discussions presented here are based on this edition. (It should be noted, too, that the overwhelming majority of Americans who read Freud do not read the *Standard Edition* but a variety of cheaper editions that reprint the earlier, inferior translations.)

The translators' tendency to replace words in ordinary use with medical terms and learned borrowings from the Greek and Latin is evident throughout the *Standard Edition*. In the tenth chapter of the *Introductory Lectures on Psychoanalysis* (1916–17), in which Freud discusses the meaning of symbols in dreams, he writes, "That the oven is [a symbol of] a woman and womb is confirmed by the Greek legend of Periander and his wife, Melissa" ("*Dass der Ofen ein Weib und Mutterleib ist, wird uns durch die griechische Sage von Periander von Korinth und seiner Frau Melissa bestätigt*"). This is rendered in the *Standard Edition* as "That ovens represent women and the uterus is confirmed by . . ." There are several difficulties here. The seemingly innocuous change from "the oven" and "a woman" to "ovens" and "women" not only is gratuitous but may make the statement untrue. I have encountered quite a few dreams in which an oven or a stove stood for a woman or for the womb, but I have never heard of a dream in which ovens represented either women or wombs in the plural. Far worse, of course, is the translation of "womb" as "uterus." I have certainly never encountered a dream in which an oven stood for a uterus, nor have any of my psychoanalyst friends. But even in the unlikely event that such dreams may occur, this is not what Freud had in mind. Though in English "womb" and "uterus" can be used interchangeably, *Mutterleib* ("mother's womb") can be translated only as "womb." The wish to substitute a medical term for a word in ordinary use leads to the replacement of a word that has deep emotional associations with one that evokes hardly any. Who would want to return to a uterus?

Freud chose the title "*Die Zerlegung der Psychischen Persönlichkeit*" for the thirty-first chapter of his *New Introductory Lectures on Psychoanalysis.* A literal translation of this title is "The Taking Apart of the Psychic Personality." Within the context of the title, *Zerlegung* ("taking apart") could be more colloquially rendered as "analysis" or "division." In the *Standard Edition* this chapter is called "The Anatomy of the Mental Personality." Nothing in the original suggests the possibility of translating *Zerlegung* as "anatomy," nor does German usage permit such translation. The word "anatomy" (*Anatomie*) is used as frequently in German as it is in English, and it has the same meaning in both languages. Freud, who studied anatomy as a medical student, would have used this word if this is what he had had in mind. The translators' choice of this word reflects their preference for using medical terms.

Only the wish to perceive psychoanalysis as a medical

specialty can explain why three of Freud's most important new theoretical concepts were translated not into English but into a language whose most familiar use today may be for writing prescriptions. Freud conceptualized the organization of the psyche by dividing its functioning into the realms of the conscious, the preconscious, and the unconscious. The psychological processes he discusses are personal and internal. In naming two of the concepts, Freud chose words that are among the first words used by every German child. To refer to the unknown, unconscious contents of the mind, he chose the personal pronoun "it" (*es*) and used it as a noun (*das Es*). But the meaning of the term "the it" gained its full impact only after Freud used it in conjunction with the pronoun "I" (*ich*), also used as a noun (*das Ich*). His intended meanings found their clear expression in the title of the book—*Das Ich und das Es*—in which he defined these two concepts for the first time, as counterparts of each other. The translation of these personal pronouns into their Latin equivalents—the "ego" and the "id" —rather than their English ones turned them into cold technical terms, which arouse no personal associations. In German, of course, the pronouns are invested with deep emotional significance, for the readers have used them all their lives; Freud's careful and original choice of words facilitated an intuitive understanding of his meaning.

No word has greater and more intimate connotations than the pronoun "I." It is one of the most frequently used words in spoken language—and, more important, it is the most *personal* word. To mistranslate *Ich* as "ego" is to transform it into jargon that no longer conveys the personal commitment we make when we say "I" or "me"—not to mention our subconscious memories of the deep emotional experience we had when, in infancy, we discovered ourselves as we learned to say "I." I do not know whether Freud was familiar with Ortega y Gasset's statement that to create a concept is to leave reality behind, but he was certainly aware of its truth and tried to avoid this danger as much as possible. In creating the concept of the *Ich*, he tied it to reality by using a term that made it practically impossible to leave reality behind. Reading or speaking about the I forces one to look at oneself introspectively. By contrast, an "ego" that uses clear-cut mechanisms, such as displacement and projection, to achieve its purpose in its struggle against the "id" is something that can be studied from the outside, by observing others. With this inappropriate and—as far as our emotional response to it is concerned—misleading translation, an introspective psychology is made into a behavioral one, which observes from the outside. This, of course, is exactly how most Americans view and use psychoanalysis.

The word "ego" was used in the English language in a number of ways long before Freud's translators introduced it as a psychoanalytic concept. These uses, which are still part of the living language, are all pejorative, such as "egoism," "egoistic," and "egotism." (A slang expression of more recent origin—"ego trip"—is also pejorative.) This is likewise true of their German cognates—the noun *Egoist* and the adjective *egoistisch*. Freud, like all German-speaking people, was, of course, familiar with the derogatory connotation of selfishness that the root "ego" evokes.

When Freud named one of his major concepts the I, he brought his theories about the workings of the human psyche as close to us, his readers, as is possible through a choice of words. If anything, the German *Ich* is invested with stronger and deeper personal meaning than the English "I." When a speaker of English wishes to emphasize personal commitment, he is apt to use "me" rather than "I." For example, he'll say, "That's me," whereas in German one would use "I," as in *"Ich bin es, der spricht"* ("That's me talking"). For that matter, a good case could be made that in some contexts "the me" might render Freud's meaning better than "the I." Where Freud selected a word that, used in daily parlance, makes us feel vibrantly alive, the translations present us with a term from a dead language that reeks of erudition precisely when it should emanate vitality.

The assertiveness we often feel when we say "I" is an image of how the person's I tries to assert its will over what in the translations are called the "id" and "superego," and over the external world. This image gets lost when we talk about an ego. When I say "I," I mean my entire self, my total personality. Freud, it is true, made an important distinction here. What he called the "I" refers primarily to the conscious, rational aspects of oneself. In a way, we know that we are not always reasonable and do not always act rationally; psychoanalysis, more than any other discipline, makes us aware of the irrational, unconscious aspects of our mind. So, when Freud names the reasonable, conscious aspects of our mind the I, we feel subtly flattered that our *real* I is what we value most highly in ourselves. It gives us the intuitive feeling that Freud is right to name the I what we feel to be our true self, even though we know that we do not always act in line with that self. Since that part of us, psychoanalytically speaking, is named the I, we are enticed to side with it in its struggle against the irrational, infantile, entirely selfish aspects of ourselves. In a subtle way, this choice of name for the conscious aspects of our mind strengthens our determination to win the battle against the chaos caused by the irrational in us. During psychoanalytic treatment, that determination—that siding of the patient's I with the efforts of the therapist—alone can lead to success in dealing with the dark forces within us. The I, more than any other term of psychoanalysis, encourages us to make the unconscious become conscious and to think psychoanalytically.

We find it easy to say, "I won't any longer be run by my irrational anxieties," and when we say it after becoming acquainted with psychoanalytic thinking we know that this I about which we speak is essentially only our conscious mind, which tries to control the anxious outcroppings of our unconscious. Nobody can say, "My ego won't any longer be run by irrational anxieties," and mean it. When we say, "I am trying to understand why I did this," our whole being is involved in the effort, although we know that it is our rational mind alone that is trying to understand why some unconscious pressure made us do something. In the most unlikely event that somebody said, "My ego is trying to understand why I did this," no feeling of personal involvement would be communicated.

"Ego" and "id" are part of a theoretical lingo, but the main purpose of psychoanalysis is to help us deal with the *least* theoretical aspects of our mind—with that in us which is most primitive, most irrational, and can be expressed, if at all, only in the most ordinary, least complicated language. The distinction between the I and the it is immediately clear to us, and hardly needs psychoanalytic explanation, since we are aware of it from our way of talking about ourselves. For example, when we say, "I went there," we know exactly what we were doing and why we did it. But when we say "It pulled me in that direction," we express the feeling that something in us—we don't know what—forced us to behave in a certain way. When a person suffering from depression says "It got me again" or "It makes life unbearable!" he gives clear expression to his feeling that neither his intellect nor his conscious mind nor his will accounts for what is happening to him—that he has been overcome by forces within him which are beyond his ken and his control.

Still, even "the it" does not have the full emotional impact that *das Es* has in the original German. In German, the word "child" (*das Kind*) is of neuter gender. During their early years, all Germans have the experience of being referred to by means of the neuter pronoun *es*. This fact gives the phrase *das Es* a special feeling, reminding the German reader that this is how he was referred to before he learned to repress many of his sexual, aggressive, and otherwise asocial impulses, before he felt guilty or ashamed because of them, before he felt an obligation to resolve contradictions and bring logical order into his thoughts; in short, it reminds him of a time when his entire existence was dominated by the it. These memories, even when he is not conscious of them, permit a much more immediate empathy with what Freud meant when he used this term for the unconscious.

The concept of the *Über-Ich*, which Freud also introduced in *Das Ich und das Es,* and which has become known to English readers as the "superego," combines two everyday German words. It is the second part of his compound noun that gives it its main significance, by emphasizing the point that the concept denotes an integral part of the person —a controlling and often overcontrolling institution of the mind which is created by the person himself out of inner needs and external pressures that have been internalized. The preposition *über* ("above," "over") removes the realm of the *Über-Ich* from the sphere of the *Ich*.

As it happens, the English mistranslation of the above-I soon became accepted and is now used in English more easily and frequently than either "ego" or "id." People who hardly ever speak about egos or ids do not hesitate to talk about their or others' superegos. The reason may be that there had been no name for that which includes not just the "conscience"—for this the old word did admirably well— but also that wider aspect of the psyche which comprises both its conscious and fairly reasonable controlling aspects and its unconscious, unreasonable, compulsive, punitive, and persecutory aspects.

In Freud's system, the I, the it, and the above-I are but different aspects of our psyche, each of them inextricably and permanently related to one another; they cannot be separated from each other except in theory. Each of them, in its own way, exercises an important and different—albeit overlapping—function in the psyche. In English transla- tion, it is not so much the "super" in "superego" that inter- feres with an emotional understanding of its meaning and its role in Freud's system; the problem, as before, is with the term "ego." The function of *Ich* as part of *Über-Ich* is to communicate as directly as a word can the idea that it is the person himself who created this controlling institution of his mind, that the above-I is the result of his own experiences, desires, needs, and anxieties, as they have been interpreted by him, and that this institution attained its role of power because he, the person, internalized in its contents the demands he made—and continues to make—of himself. Through such a personal realization, it is readily understood that others have done the same, and that the above-I plays the same role in their psyches. Had "I" been retained as the most significant part of the name given to what was instead misnamed "superego," a reader would find it much easier to get an immediate feeling that it is he who has to contend with this part of his psyche. All that the qualifying part of the compound word needs to convey is that it refers to those aspects of the psyche which attempt to rule the person through a claim of higher authority. In this respect, "above-I," "over-I," "upper-I," and other, similar terms would all be acceptable translations of *Über-Ich*. "Upper-I" might even come closest to the meaning Freud had in mind. One of the definitions of "upper" given in *Webster's New World Dictionary of the American Language* (henceforth referred to as *Webster's*) is "higher in authority, something above another similar thing, or a related part." We are all familiar with the concept of an upper house, which has (usually) greater authority than a lower house. The connotations of a location that is higher up, and at the same time superior and of a higher authority, are exactly those that made Freud choose the word *über*.

Translations of Freud into languages other than English show that there was no compelling reason—except an unconscious desire to create emotional distance from the impact that personal pronouns have, or to use as much as possible the special language of medicine—for having recourse to Latin pronouns in translating into English the

German pronouns that Freud used. In French translations of Freud, *das Ich* is nearly always rendered as *le moi*; *das Es* is rendered as *le ça* or *le soi*; and the *Über-Ich* is *le surmoi*. In Spanish, *das Ich* is translated as *el yo*.

In *The Question of Lay Analysis*, Freud defended his use of personal pronouns in naming the different aspects of the psyche, and gave his reasons for rejecting words of a classical language for this purpose. Speaking to an imaginary interlocutor, he wrote:

> You will probably object to our having chosen simple pronouns to denote our two institutions, or provinces, of the soul, instead of introducing for them sonorous Greek names. In psychoanalysis, however, we like to keep in contact with the popular mode of thinking and prefer to make its concepts scientifically serviceable rather than to discard them. There is no special merit in this; we must proceed in this way because our teachings ought to be comprehensible to our patients who are often very intelligent, but not always learned. The impersonal "it" is immediately connected with certain expressions used by normal persons. One is apt to say, "It came to me in a flash; there was something in me which, at that moment, was stronger than me." "*C'était plus fort que moi.*"

In the paragraph preceding the one just quoted, Freud explained that he chose to name one of the concepts the I because of the common connotations that are attached to this pronoun. He wrote:

We base ourselves on common knowledge and recognize in man an organization of the soul which is interpolated between the stimulation of his senses and the perception of his bodily needs on the one hand, and his motor acts on the other, and which mediates between them for a particular purpose. We call this organization his I. Now there is nothing new in this; each of us makes this assumption without being a philosopher, and some although they are philosophers. But we don't believe that by recognizing this part of the apparatus of the soul we have exhausted the description. Besides the I we recognize also another region of the soul, more extensive, grander, and more obscure than the I, and this we call the it.

Nietzsche, who indeed used the words "I" and "it" in a similar way, may be one of the philosophers Freud alluded to here. In *Beyond Good and Evil*, Nietzsche wrote, "A thought comes when 'it' wants to and not when 'I' want; thus it is a falsification to say: the subject 'I' is the condition for the predicate 'think.' It thinks: but there is . . . no immediate certainty that this 'it' is just that famous old 'I.' "

Late in his life, Freud updated his thoughts on the structure of the human psyche in the thirty-first of the *New Introductory Lectures on Psychoanalysis*. At its conclusion, he summed up the purpose of psychoanalysis as theory and as therapy with the statement "Where it was, there should become I." By this he did not mean that the I should eliminate the it or take over the it's place in our psyche, since according to his theoretical constructs the it is the source of our vital energy, without which life itself could not continue. ("The it cannot be controlled beyond certain limits," Freud wrote in *Civilization and Its Discontents*. "If more is demanded of a man, a revolt will be produced in him or a neurosis, or he will be made unhappy.") Freud's statement in the *New Introductory Lectures* was meant to indicate that in some instances, with respect to certain aspects of life that have been previously dominated entirely or largely by the it, the I ought to exercise its constructive influence and successfully control the undesirable outcroppings of the it. The task of psychoanalysis is thus to allow the I to make additional inroads into the vast realm of the it, and to help the I gain ascendancy particularly over those aspects of the it which can disturb the person's well-being.

It was so important to Freud to make clear what he meant by his statement about the goal of psychoanalysis that he followed it with one final paragraph, consisting of a single sentence: "It is a cultural achievement somewhat like the draining of the Zuyder Zee." This is an especially apt simile. The reclamation of the Zuyder Zee area involved controlling, damming up, and draining a fairly large inlet of the North Sea. The sea is a primordial, dominant element of the natural world, comparable to the it in the world of the psyche. The sea is not only the element in which all life began, but it is necessary for life's continuance. When the Zuyder Zee project was completed, only a tiny part of the vast North Sea had been pushed back. The project has remained a precarious achievement, because the reclaimed land has to be continuously protected against renewed flooding. A furious onslaught of the elements, such as a huge tidal wave, could undo much of what has been accomplished. The parallels here to the it in relation to the I, and to the work of psychoanalysis, are obvious.

The draining of the Zuyder Zee was a technical achievement, and in order to make it suitable as a metaphor for what he had in mind, Freud added an important qualification. He declared it a *cultural* achievement. He used the word *Kulturarbeit*, which means, literally, "labor to achieve culture." In the *Standard Edition* this term is rendered as "reclamation work." By no stretch of the imagination can "reclamation work" be viewed as an appropriate translation of *Kulturarbeit*. If Freud had not wished to evoke the work done at the Zuyder Zee in a particular metaphoric sense, but had wished simply to refer to its nature and purpose, he would have used the word *Urbarmachung*, which is the correct German expression for the reclamation of land for agricultural purposes. But Freud was not concerned with comparing psychoanalysis to the work of reclamation; on the contrary, he wanted psychoanalysis to be compared to the wresting away from primordial elements of areas that could be made available for cultural achievement. In his metaphor, Freud wished to stress that the work of psychoanalysis is spiritual, as distinguished from physical or material work. The English translation gives the metaphor the opposite meaning and makes it seem that the purpose of psychoanalytic work is to gain practical results. Whatever practical benefits may be derived from psychoanalysis, they are only incidental to its cultural achievements, which were paramount to Freud, and on which he rested his case.

For those familiar with German culture there is a special poignancy in Freud's summing up the essence of psychoanalysis with a metaphor based on the reclamation of land from the sea. In the history of German culture nobody looms larger than Goethe, whose masterpiece is *Faust*. The story of Faust is that of a battle for his soul between the forces of light and darkness. His life is a struggle for a deeper understanding of the world and himself. To discover who he is, Faust is willing to risk everything —his life, even his soul. In Faust's struggle, his better self is in conflict with powerful and sometimes overwhelming instinctual pressures (embodied in Mephistopheles) that lead to the destruction of what he loves most (embodied in Gretchen). Gretchen represents Faust's better self; it is she, and what she represents, that saves Faust's soul. At the end of his life, Faust views the reclamation of a piece of land from the sea as the crowning achievement of his strivings. Believing that he has achieved this work, he is contented and ready to end his restless life. Because of his efforts to create new land for future cultivation, he finds salvation. Since we know that Goethe played a dominant role in Freud's intellectual development, it is not mere speculation that Freud selected the metaphor of the reclamation of land from the sea because it would induce the reader to relate the work of psychoanalysis to *Faust*, the great poem about the reclamation of the soul. The image of the saving of the soul is one without which neither the pantheist Goethe nor the atheist Freud felt able to convey his deepest thoughts about man's destiny.

IX

The most important of Freud's psychoanalytic works is *The Interpretation of Dreams*. In this book he tried to elucidate what goes on in our unconscious and our dreams, and he proved the truth of Shakespeare's statement that "we are such stuff as dreams are made on." Unfortunately, beginning with the title, mistranslations hamper our grasp of this important work.

The Interpretation of Dreams, while not literally an incorrect translation of *Die Traumdeutung*, is by no means a felicitous rendering of what the German title conveys. The two nouns in the English title have exact counterparts in German. "Dream" and *Traum* are equivalent. "Interpretation" is a German word as well as an English one, and if it had been the word Freud had in mind for his title, he would have used it; or he could have chosen a similar German word, such as *Erklärung* (explanation). He preferred to use instead a word that has quite different meanings and connotations than "interpretation" has in either German or English.

The authoritative *Duden*, which does for the German language what the *Oxford English Dictionary* (OED) does for English, explains that *Deutung* means an "attempt to grasp the deeper sense or the significance of something" (*Versuch den tieferen Sinn, die Bedeutung von etwas zu erfassen*). This, then, is what Freud wished to convey by his title: that what he was presenting was an *attempt* at *grasping* for a *deeper* sense. The first sentence of his introduction to the book emphasizes this idea; it begins: "In here attempting a presentation of the meaning of dreams . . ." (or, since the German word he uses is again *Traumdeutung*, one might replace "meaning" with "deeper meaning"). *Deutung* is derived from the verbs *deuten* and *bedeuten*, and the connotations of these verbs adhere to the noun. *Duden* defines *deuten* as "to point with a finger at something," and its definition of *bedeuten* includes: "what is its sense, what does it mean, what is behind it, what is at the bottom of it" (*welchen Sinn hat das, was meint es, was steckt dahinter*).

What Freud intended to indicate with the title *Die Traumdeutung* was that he would attempt to point out the many-layered nature of dreams, to elucidate their meaning by showing what lay behind them. He did not mean to promise that he would be able to "make clear and explicit" (the OED's definition of "interpret") the meaning of dreams, because that would be impossible. Every dream has many elements. First, there is the manifest dream, the dream remembered. Behind it is the latent dream content, of which the manifest dream is only a remnant or a distortion. There is also the day residue, some recent experience that is woven into the dream, or that partly causes it. And there are wishes that find expression in the dream, as well as many other unconscious elements. Freud was indeed trying to show what lies behind the dream as it is remembered on awakening, and this search for what is at the bottom of the dream (*was steckt dahinter*) is implied in the word *Deutung*.

The difference between the English word "interpretation" and the German word *Deutung* is best suggested by another German compound word: *Sterndeutung* (astrology). Both *Sterndeutung* and *Traumdeutung* signify most ancient efforts to make sense of something—in the first case, the movements of the stars; in the second, dreams. There are parallels between these ancient efforts to discover meaning and the entirely new efforts of Freud. Astrologers try to predict the future from events long past, since the movements of the stars and constellations on which they base their predictions occurred light-years ago. Soothsayers and dream interpreters also rely on supposed ancient wisdom, such as that handed down from the Egyptians (probably chosen because of Joseph's predictions based on Pharaoh's dreams). Freud shared with these practitioners the conviction that guided his pioneering discoveries: that dreams have important meaning and that we can discover this meaning. He agreed that to a large extent dreams can be understood only as the consequence of past events—not events in the heavens, however, but those of individual human lives. In a way, he turned the beliefs of astrologers and dream interpreters upside down: he showed that through the interpretation of dreams we cannot predict the future but can indeed discover otherwise unknown events of the past.

By giving his book a title that he knew must evoke associations to the ancient but still popular superstitious and fantastic attempts to make sense of incomprehensible phenomena, Freud indicated that he did not shun efforts to make sense out of what all serious-minded, scientifically inclined people were convinced was utter nonsense. His title suggests, too, that when analyzing dreams one cannot expect to arrive at anything close to the definitive certainty required in the natural sciences. In his paper "A Difficulty of Psychoanalysis"[1] (1917), Freud compared his discovery of psychoanalysis to the work of Copernicus, who, starting as an astrologer, founded modern astronomy—the discipline that completely changed our views of the universe and gave us an understanding of what goes on in the infinite (or possibly finite, but nevertheless unimaginably vast) outer space within which all of life unfolds. Freud believed that the study and understanding of our dreams would open to our comprehension the previously unrecognized enormous inner space of the soul.

The Latin motto that precedes the text further warns that the book deals with a murky world, where one cannot expect the level of clarity that an "interpretation" would offer. The motto—which Freud settled on only after much hesitation and deliberation about the suitability of other quotations—is a line from Virgil's *Aeneid*: *Flectere si nequeo Superos, Acheronta movebo*. The significance of this motto is lost on anyone who is not familiar with Latin and Latin literature. Even a translation—"If I cannot move heaven, I will stir up the underworld"—fails to communicate the full meaning; one needs also to know the context in which the line occurs. In Virgil's poem, Juno speaks these words in

[1]While not actually mistranslating the title of this paper, the translator added three entirely superfluous words to it. Freud titled the essay *"Eine Schwierigkeit der Psychoanalyse,"* which simply means "a difficulty of psychoanalysis." The difficulty he discusses is the blow psychoanalysis inflicts on our narcissism by showing that our I is not master of its own house. This injury to our self-love Freud compares to that which Copernicus inflicted by showing us that the earth is not the center of the universe, and to that which Darwin inflicted by forcing us to recognize how closely we are related to other animals. The title of this essay is given in the *Standard Edition* as "A Difficulty in the Path of Psychoanalysis," although nowhere in the paper does Freud speak of a "path" of psychoanalysis that some difficulty would obstruct.

desperation because she has failed to get help from the gods and thus must seek it from the infernal regions. Read in this context, the motto suggests that only when aid from the powers of light (the conscious mind) is insufficient or unavailable are we justified in calling on the powers of darkness (the unconscious) for help in gaining our goals (in this case, an understanding of dreams). This motto is particularly appropriate because it can also be read to suggest that if the superior world (our conscious mind) refuses to respond to the unconscious, then the underworld of the unconscious will shake up this superior world. Thus, the motto, like the word *Deutung*, warns that we shall have to enter a world of darkness and uncertainty, a world of chaos that defies clearcut translation and interpretation.

By inviting us to follow him into the seeming chaos of the world of darkness, of the unconscious and its irrationality, Freud intended to change our views of man; but this could be done only if we changed our view of ourselves and reached an understanding also of the darkest aspects of our minds. If we did, we would discover that what went on there could be understood and would, in its own way, make good sense, teaching us a great deal about ourselves. Freud tried to correct and enlarge our ideas about our dreams and to instruct us about their meaning, hoping that familiarity with the hidden aspects of our souls would permit us a deeper, more complete understanding of ourselves.

It would be difficult to find an English title as short, concise, and evocative as *Die Traumdeutung*, a title that would indicate all this at a glance to the casual reader. But "interpretation," with its implied promise of a clearcut and definite explanation of dreams, is misleading. It promises too much and makes things appear much less ambiguous than they are in reality. Titles such as *A Search for the Meaning of Dreams* or *An Inquiry into the Meaning of Dreams*, while awkward, would have been more in line with what Freud wished to convey. Soon after the appearance of his book on dreams, Freud had a fantasy that he reported in a letter to his friend Fliess. This fantasy was that someday a marble tablet would mark the place where he understood for the first time the meaning of dreams; it would bear the inscription "Here the secret of dreams was revealed to Dr. Sigmund Freud on July 24, 1895." Thus, Freud could have named his book *The Secret of Dreams.* But he did not. He chose instead a title that would suggest a beginning, and that would give the impression that his book dealt with the ancient pseudoscience of dream interpretation and would even evoke associations to that other equally ancient pseudoscience, astrology. The English title gives the impression that Freud presented a definitive treatise on dreams; by failing to summon associations to astrology, it does not suggest the parallel between the discovery of the true nature of the universe and the discovery of the true inner world of the soul.

X

Of all the mistranslations of Freud's phraseology, none has hampered our understanding of his humanistic views more than the elimination of his references to the soul (*die Seele*).

Freud evokes the image of the soul quite frequently—especially in crucial passages where he is attempting to provide a broad view of his system. For instance, in *The Interpretation of Dreams*, where he is discussing the origin of dreams, he states "that the dream is a result of the activity of our own soul" ("*dass der Traum ein Ergebnis unserer eigenen Seelentätigkeit ist*"). And in *The Question of Lay Analysis*, where he is conceptualizing the workings of the psyche, distinguishing the conscious from the unconscious, and distinguishing the functions of the it, the I, and the above-I, he uses the term "soul" to describe what he regards as the overarching concept that takes in all the others. It seems natural to Freud to speak of man's soul. By evoking the image of the soul and all its associations, Freud is emphasizing our common humanity. Unfortunately, even in these crucial passages the translations make us believe that he is talking about our mind, our intellect. This is particularly misleading because we often view our intellectual life as set apart from—and even opposed to—our emotional life, the life of our fantasies and dreams. The goal of psychoanalysis, of course, is to integrate the emotional life into the intellectual life.

In various places, Freud spoke about "the structure of the soul" and "the organization of the soul" ("*die Struktur des seelischen Apparats*" and "*die seelische Organisation*"). In the translation, these terms are almost always rendered as "mental apparatus" or "mental organization." Such substitutions are particularly misleading because in German the words *Seele* and *seelisch* have even more exclusively spiritual meanings than the word "soul" has in present-day American usage. The word that the translators substitute for "of the soul"—"mental"—has an exact German equivalent; namely, *geistig*, which means "of the mind," or "of the intellect." If Freud had meant *geistig*, he would have written *geistig*.

I will let a few examples speak for many. In the *New Introductory Lectures on Psychoanalysis*, in the chapter entitled "The Analysis of the Psychical Personality," Freud, speaking of the I, the it, and the above-I, describes them as "the three provinces of the apparatus of the soul" ("*die drei Provinzen des seelischen Apparats*"). In the *Standard Edition* the phrase is translated as "the three provinces of the mental apparatus." Further on in that chapter, Freud remarks on "*die Strukturverhältnisse der seelischen Persönlichkeit.*" The phrase is admittedly difficult to translate; a literal rendering would require referring to "the personality of the soul." Probably the best way to convey Freud's meaning would be something on the order of "the structural relations of the innermost personality, or soul." The *Standard Edition* gives us "the structural relations of the mental personality." In the first chapter of the *New Introductory Lectures*, Freud writes about the conflict that dominates the processes going on in our souls: "You know . . . that the conflict between two psychical agencies which we—inaccurately—designate as the unconscious that is fended off and the conscious altogether dominates the life of our soul." ("*Sie wissen . . . dass der Konflikt zweier psychischer Instanzen, die wir—ungenau—als das unbewusst Verdrängte und das Bewusste bezeichnen, überhaupt unser Seelenleben beherrscht.*"). In the *Standard Edition*, "dominates the life of our soul" becomes "dominates our whole mental life." Freud concludes his preface to the *New Introductory Lectures* with a remark about "whoever loves the science of the life of the soul" ("*wer die Wissenschaft vom Seelenleben liebt"*). He is clearly referring to psychoanalysis, to himself, and to the imaginary listeners he had in mind when preparing this series of lectures, which were never intended to be given. This passage could easily be rendered as "whoever loves psychoanalysis" or "whoever loves psychology." Instead, it is translated as "whoever cares for the science of mental life."

Almost invariably, the *Standard Edition* (like the earlier English translations) either omits Freud's references to the soul or translates them as if he spoke only of man's mind. In the paper "The 'Uncanny' " (1919), Freud's phrase *"im seelischen Unbewussten"* ("in the unconscious of the soul") has been translated as "in the unconscious mind." In the same sentence, *"gewisse Seiten des Seelenlebens"* ("certain aspects of the life of the soul") has been rendered as "certain aspects of the mind."

Freud never faltered in his conviction that it was important to think in terms of the soul when trying to comprehend his system, because no other concept could make equally clear what he meant; nor can there be any doubt that he meant the soul, and not the mind, when he wrote *"seelisch."* As early as 1905, in the opening passage of an article entitled "Psychical Treatment (Treatment of the Soul)," he wrote:

> "Psyche" is a Greek word and its German translation is "soul." Psychical treatment hence means "treatment of the soul." One could thus think that what is meant is: treatment of the morbid phenomena in the life of the soul. But this is not the meaning of this term. Psychical treatment wishes to signify,

rather, treatment originating in the soul, treatment—
of psychic or bodily disorders—by measures which
influence above all and immediately the soul of man.

*(Psyche ist ein griechisches Wort und lautet in
deutscher Übersetzung Seele. Psychische Behandlung
heisst demnach Seelenbehandlung. Man könnte also
meinen, dass darunter verstanden wird: Behandlung der
krankhaften Erscheinungen des Seelenlebens. Dies ist
aber nicht die Bedeutung dieses Wortes. Psychische Behandlung will vielmehr besagen: Behandlung von der
Seele aus, Behandlung—seelischer oder körperlicher Stö-
rungen—mit Mitteln, welche zunächst und unmittelbar
auf das Seelische des Menschen einwirken.)*

In the *Standard Edition*, the title of the paper is given
as "Psychical (or Mental) Treatment," and the passage is
translated:

"Psyche" is a Greek word which may be translated "mind." Thus "psychical treatment" means
"mental treatment." The term might accordingly be
supposed to signify "treatment of the pathological
phenomena of mental life." This, however, is *not* its
meaning. "Psychical treatment" denotes, rather,
treatment taking its start in the mind, treatment
(whether of mental or physical disorders) by measures which operate in the first instance and immediately upon the human mind.

In a footnote, the translators acknowledge that *Seele* is "a
word which is in fact nearer to the Greek 'psyche' than is

the English 'mind.' " By failing to mention that the English word for *Seele* is "soul," not "mind," the footnote merely distorts Freud's emphatic statement even further.

In *An Outline of Psychoanalysis*, written in 1938 and published posthumously in 1940, Freud emphasized that his life's work had been devoted to understanding as fully as possible the world of man's soul. He had repeatedly stated that the I is only one aspect of our psyche, or soul, and separated it from the two others, the it and the above-I. Perhaps at this juncture it seemed particularly important to him to make clear that when he was speaking of what pertains to the I he meant our conscious mental life, and that when he was referring to all three institutions, to the mind in its totality, to our conscious and our unconscious life, he spoke of our soul. "Psychoanalysis," he wrote, "makes a basic assumption whose discussion is reserved to philosophical thought but whose justification lies in its results. We know two kinds of things about what we call our psyche (the life of the soul) [*Von dem, was wir unsere Psyche (Seelenleben) nennen, ist uns zweierlei bekannt*]." This passage makes it abundantly clear that for Freud the psyche and the life of the soul are the same thing. As usual, the *Standard Edition* translates the reference to the soul as if it referred to the mind: "We know two kinds of things about what we call our psyche (or mental life)."

In an early version of *An Outline of Psychoanalysis*, under the title *Some Elementary Lessons in Psycho-Analysis*, Freud wrote, "Psychoanalysis is a part of psychology which is dedicated to the science of the soul" (*"Die Psychoanalyse ist ein Stück der Seelenkunde der Psychologie"*). For Freud, psychology is the large discipline, part of which is the science of the soul; psychoanalysis is a special division of the latter discipline. It is hard to think of a statement that could more strongly assert that psychoanalysis is essentially concerned with man's soul. In the *Standard Edition*, the sentence reads: "Psychoanalysis is a part of the mental science of psychology."

There really was no reason—apart from a wish to interpret psychoanalysis as a medical specialty—for this corruption of Freud's references to the soul. There was no reason for the English translators to misunderstand these references. The first three definitions of the word "soul" given in *The Shorter Oxford English Dictionary* express very well what Freud had in mind. The first definition, "the principle of life in man," is declared to be obsolete, and is quoted only for the sake of completeness. The second and third definitions, "the spiritual part of man in contrast to the purely physical" and "the emotional part of man's nature," are most pertinent. It is true that in common American usage the word "soul" has been more or less restricted to the sphere of religion. This was not the case in Freud's Vienna, and it is not the case in German-speaking countries today. In German the word *Seele* has retained its full meaning as man's essence, as that which is most spiritual and worthy in man. *Seele* ought to have been translated in this sense.

What Freud considered as forming or pertaining to the essence of man, man's soul, the translators have relegated entirely to the I, the thinking and reasoning part of man. They have disregarded the nonthinking it, the irrational world of the unconscious and of the emotions. Freud uses *Seele* and *seelisch* rather than *geistig* because *geistig* refers mainly to the rational aspects of the mind, to that of which we are conscious. The idea of the soul, by contrast, definitely includes much of which we are not consciously aware. Freud wanted to make clear that psychoanalysis was concerned not just with man's body and his intellect, as his medical colleagues were, but—and most of all—with the dark world of the unconscious which forms such a large part of the soul of living man—or, to put it in classical terms, with that unknown netherworld in which, according to ancient myths, the souls of men dwell.

Nowhere in his writings does Freud give us a precise definition of the term "soul." I suspect that he chose the term *because* of its inexactitude, its emotional resonance. Its ambiguity speaks for the ambiguity of the psyche itself, which reflects many different, warring levels of consciousness simultaneously. To have attempted a clinical definition of such a term—a definition that Freud's English translators would no doubt have welcomed—would have robbed it of its value as an expression of Freud's thinking. I should point out, however, that when Freud speaks of the soul he is talking not about a religious phenomenon but about a psychological concept; it too is a metaphor. Freud's atheism is well known—he went out of his way to assert it. There is nothing supernatural about his idea of the soul, and it has nothing to do with immortality; if anything endures after us, it is other people's memories of us—and what we create. By "soul" or "psyche" Freud means that which is most valuable in man while he is alive. Freud was a passionate man. For him, the soul is the seat both of the mind and of the passions, and we remain largely unconscious of the soul. In important respects, it is deeply hidden, hardly accessible even to careful investigation. It is intangible, but it nevertheless exercises a powerful influence on our lives. It is what makes us human; in fact, it is what is so essentially human about us that no other term could equally convey what Freud had in mind.

XI

Others before me have criticized the English translations of Freud's writings, but such criticism has been very rare and confined, in most cases, to a few short sentences, as if this were a topic to avoid. Edoardo Weiss, in his book *Principles of Psychodynamics* (1950), remarked: ". . . the body as well as the mind of the individual is experienced in the 'I,' one may add that neither is experienced in the 'ego'!" Max Schur discussed other mistranslations, some of which I quote here, in *Freud: Living and Dying* (1972). Lewis J. Brandt devoted to the subject an entire (though quite short) article, "Some Notes on English Freudian Terminology,"[1] and H. Frank Brull did the same, in "A Reconsideration of Some Translations of Sigmund Freud";[2] Brull is, to my knowledge, the only person who has taken the translators to task for misrendering Freud's references to man's soul. Ernest Jones,

[1] *Journal of the American Psychoanalytic Association*, 1961.
[2] *Psychotherapy: Theory, Research and Practice*, 12, 1975.

Freud's associate and biographer, declared that some of the translations "were not only seriously inaccurate" but "unworthy of Freud's style and gave a misleading impression of his personality."[3] Jones reports that when he remarked to Freud that it was "a pity" his work was not being presented to the English-speaking world in "a more worthy form," Freud replied, "I'd rather have a good friend than a good translator."

Freud's lack of interest in how he was mistranslated in English can perhaps be explained by his general animus toward things American, an animosity that was certainly fed by the American insistence that psychoanalysis be considered a medical specialty. Freud expressed his negative feelings most vividly when he told Ernest Jones, "America is gigantic, but it is a gigantic mistake." We cannot be sure why Freud thought so, but—apart from whatever unknown personal reasons he had for making this remark—his views must have been influenced by what he regarded as the American commitment to materialism and technological accomplishments, which excluded those cultural—one may say spiritual—values that were most important to him.

In the chapter of *An Outline of Psychoanalysis* entitled "Psychical Qualities," Freud wrote, "The starting-point for this investigation is provided by a fact without parallel, which defies all explanation or description—the fact of consciousness. Nevertheless, if anyone speaks of consciousness, we know immediately and from our most personal experi-

[3]In his book *Free Associations* (New York: Basic Books, 1959).

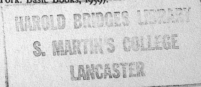

ence what is meant by it." To this statement he appended a footnote that neither the text nor the context required: "One extreme line of thought, such as the doctrine of behaviorism which originated in America, believes it possible to construct a psychology which disregards this fundamental fact!" Freud was disgusted by a civilization that could explicitly deny the phenomenon of consciousness. He was also dismayed by what he recognized as the prevalence of a shallow optimism in the United States, which stood in stark contrast to his own tragic and essentially pessimistic view of life. But if Freud had put into words what he held most against the United States, he might have said that America was lacking in soul.

Freud came close to expressing these ideas in *Civilization and Its Discontents.* At one point in this book he warned that a condition may arise which might be termed "the psychological misery of the masses" ("*das psychologische Elend der Masse*"), and he added, "The present cultural state of America would give a good opportunity for studying this feared damage to culture. But I shall avoid the temptation of entering upon a critique of American culture. I do not wish to give the impression of wanting to employ American methods myself." Freud failed to specify what "American methods" he was so critical of that he would not deign to employ them. But it is clear that he thought the state of American culture causes psychological misery.

The English version of this passage provides one of many examples of mistranslations that considerably weaken the force of what Freud said. The German word *Elend* means "misery" or "wretchedness"; but the *Standard Edi-*

tion renders Freud's phrase as "the psychological poverty of groups." (The mistranslation of *Masse* as "groups" occurs elsewhere, too; it is discussed later.) The German word for "poverty" is *Armut*, not *Elend*. Although extreme poverty can, to be sure, cause misery or wretchedness, it is by no means identical with them. The English translation permits no interpretation other than that Freud had a psychological depletion in mind, when in fact he was projecting a state of wretchedness. A word that evokes a strong emotional response, as does "misery" or "wretchedness," has been replaced with a different word that is likely to be considered as referring to an objective fact.

This tendency toward understatement is not restricted to the translation of Freud's psychological works but also mars that of his correspondence and the image of Freud the person that may be gained from reading it. For example, in a letter to Wilhelm Fliess, Freud described how, during his childhood, he and a playmate had treated his little niece cruelly. The word *grausam* (cruelly) is translated as "shockingly." While to treat a little girl cruelly may indeed be shocking, translating *grausam* as "shockingly" replaces a statement that reveals the passion causing the behavior with a moral judgment on this behavior. The original gives us a clear sense of the emotion that was involved, and the translation does not. Another example of this penchant for understatement, which weakens Freud's meaning beyond recognition and deprives his statements of their emotional impact, is found in a passage where Freud speaks about *Unheil* (disaster). In the translation, "disaster" is reduced to "trouble."

XII

Of all Freud's books, none had such an immediate success as *The Psychopathology of Everyday Life* (1901), and it has retained its popularity. In it, he discusses why we make mistakes in talking, in writing, in remembering, in handling things, and so on. The examples he uses are difficult to translate, and so are his explanations of the possible subconscious motives for making such mistakes, particularly since the explanations often involve a play on words, which does not lend itself to translation. Therefore, the translators cannot be blamed for not doing justice to the subtleties of Freud's analyses here. Nonetheless, one would expect the translators to have exercised the greatest care to avoid mistakes insofar as it was possible to do so. The very topic of the book, one would think, ought to have alerted them to their own propensity to mistranslate out of subconscious motives.

The book's title has been correctly rendered into English, with the exception of its first word. If the English title were correct, the original would have to be *Die Psychopathologie des Alltagslebens*—a very good German title, concise, straightforward, idiomatic, pungent. But this is not what Freud called the book; his title is *Zur Psychopathologie des Alltagslebens*. The German word *zur* is a frequently used contraction of *zu der* (to the). In context, *zur* is an elliptical expression of a phrase such as "A contribution to the . . ." or "Reflections on the . . ." It is best translated as "on the."

Hence, a correct translation of the title would be *On the Psychopathology of Everyday Life*—a perfectly good English title. Perhaps the translators wished to keep the title as simple, direct, and short as possible, although "The" is hardly much shorter than "On the." But even if this were their motive, it could not extend to repeating the same type of mistranslation in the subtitle, *Über Vergessen, Versprechen, Vergreifen, Aberglaube und Irrtum*. The translators did not change the first word of the subtitle; they simply dropped it. Their subtitle is "Forgetting, Slips of the Tongue, Bungled Actions, Superstitions and Errors." Freud could have used *über* (about) rather than *zur* (on) in the main title. By choosing instead to use both words, he was apparently trying to make doubly sure that the reader would recognize that the book was only *about* all these topics, and by no means an apodictic treatise on the subject.

The form into which this English title and subtitle were cast claims certainty where Freud preferred to express some hesitation. It is this hesitation that makes it easier to follow his expositions, brings his attempts closer to the reader, who feels that what he is reading is an effort to grapple with difficult problems. If the reader has doubts, he is not required to give them up immediately, and this makes what he is reading more emotionally acceptable. The unqualified English title and subtitle fail to build such an emotional bond between author and reader. They make Freud sound much more definite and assertive than he meant to be. What Freud tried to convey with his "On" and "About" is what he stated often, and much more explicitly, in other contexts. He once remarked in conversation, for example, that it is "a false assumption that the validity of psychoanalytic findings and theories are definitely established, while actually they are still in their beginning, and need a great deal of development and repeated verification and confirmation."[1] Particularly in a book devoted to errors we make not because of a lack of knowledge or skill, but because of the interference of unconscious processes, there is need for hesitation and uncertainty. As Freud understood, it is impossible to know everything that goes into making the mistake, because the unconscious itself is too varied and many-layered, too chaotic, ambiguous, ill-defined.

In his subtitle Freud mentioned five distinct groups, or examples, of errors we are apt to make when our unconscious plays tricks on us. The translations of three of them —"forgetting," "superstitions," and "errors"—are as close to the original as one could wish for. "Slips of the tongue" is an acceptable translation of *Versprechen*, but this English phrase evokes a feeling that it was the tongue itself that was responsible for the error. "Lapse" would have been a better choice. According to the OED, a "lapse" is "a slip of memory, tongue, or pen; a slight error." Freud himself used *lapsus*, the Latin word from which "lapse" is derived, as the term for some of his examples. Translating *Versprechen* as "lapse" would have another advantage: it would evoke association to the word's additional meaning as a falling away from a higher standard (in our case, from consciousness). That "a slip of the tongue" is a less than ideal translation here is also suggested by the frequency with which people

[1]Martin W. Peck, "A Brief Visit with Freud." *Psychoanalytic Quarterly*, IX, 1940.

use the expression "a Freudian slip," rather than saying either "a slip of the tongue" or "a Freudian slip of the tongue."

It would have been nice if the translators had responded to the way Freud bound together the main topics discussed in the book by using words with the same prefix, "*ver-*" (meaning "mis-"): *Vergessen, Versprechen, Vergreifen*. This usage clearly indicates that in all three cases the same thing has happened, something has gone awry in the same way or out of parallel causes. All three are instances of unconscious processes interfering with what the conscious mind wishes to achieve.

The closest one can come to the German *vergreifen* is probably the English verb "to mishandle," which has exactly the same connotation of abuse that the German word has. In addition, both the German *greifen* and the English "to handle" mean "to grasp in one's hand," and so the two prefixed words share this important connotation: something that should have been handled right has instead been handled in a wrong way. In Freud's examples of *Vergreifen*, he shows how he mishandled objects for unconscious reasons. For instance, he tells how he kicked a slipper off his foot in such a way that it broke a marble statue of Venus, and he explains that his unconscious purpose was to make a sacrifice of a valuable object in honor of the recovery of a person he loved. Far from being bungled or clumsy, this action shows great dexterity. But it is also a mishandling of an object in line with both meanings of the word: of handling something the wrong way (the slipper) and of abusing an object (the statue). Freud describes how in similar fashion, through a movement of his hand, he broke an Egyptian clay figurine.

He says that his unconscious hope was that by arranging for some small loss, a big loss might be averted. Thus, "bungled actions" as a translation of *Vergreifen* is wrong on many levels. It is wrong because the action that takes place is by no means bungled; on the contrary, it is often very clever in giving physical expression to unconscious thoughts, needs, or desires. The translation is wrong also because it gives the impression that an action was intended but clumsily executed, when often no action whatsoever was intended. The translation not only fails to give the correct meaning of the word Freud used, but it interferes with the idea that these actions, though unintended, are very skillful and goal-directed, and it obstructs the connotations of abuse that are inherent in both *Vergreifen* and the English word "mishandling."

Much more important than how the terms used to designate the various types of *Fehlleistungen* are translated is how this term itself—the central concept expounded in the book—is rendered into English. Freud coined *Fehlleistung* to signify a phenomenon that he had recognized—one that is common to the various ways in which our unconscious manages to prevail over our conscious intentions in everyday occurrences. The term combines two common, strangely opposite nouns, with which everybody has immediate and significant association. *Leistung* has the basic meaning of accomplishment, achievement, performance, which is qualified by the *Fehl* to indicate an achievement that somehow failed—was off the mark, in error. What happens in *Fehlleistung* is simultaneously—albeit on different levels of consciousness—a real achievement and a howling mistake. Normally, when we think of a mistake we feel that something has gone wrong, and when we refer to an accomplishment we approve of it. In *Fehlleistung*, the two responses become somehow merged: we both approve and disapprove, admire and disdain. *Fehlleistung* is much more than an abstract concept; it's a term that gives German readers an immediate, intuitive feeling of admiration for the cleverness and ingenuity of the unconscious processes without the readers' losing sight of the fact that the end result of those processes is a mistake. For example, when we make an error in talking we frequently feel that what we said is right, though we also somehow know it is wrong. When we forget an appointment, say, we know that forgetting it was an error, but also feel that somehow we probably wanted to avoid keeping the appointment. Perhaps the best rendering of *Fehlleistung* would be "faulty achievement." In the *Standard Edition*, *Fehlleistung* is translated as "parapraxis."

The word "parapraxis" appears for the first time in the *Standard Edition* in the editor's introduction to *The Psychopathology of Everyday Life*. Strachey writes, "We find the first mention by Freud of a parapraxis in a letter to Fliess," and he footnotes the word "parapraxis" as follows: "In German '*Fehlleistung*,' 'faulty function.' It is a curious fact that before Freud wrote this book the general concept seems not to have existed in psychology, and in English a new word had to be invented to cover it." Why a curious fact? Freud frequently felt compelled to create new concepts to convey his ideas. Secondly, *Fehlleistung* was indeed a new word, but it combined two well-known German words. Finally, "parapraxis" is not an English word.

Why "parapraxis"? Why a combination of Greek words to which the reader has no emotional response except annoyance at being presented with a basically incomprehensible word? It seems impossible to say spontaneously, "This was a parapraxis." An educated German, even if he was not very conversant with psychoanalysis, might readily say, "This was a *Fehlleistung*," but in all my years in this country I have never heard an American psychoanalyst use the word "parapraxis" in a casual conversation. I've heard it used only as a technical term, and then only rarely—and always by someone speaking about a patient, not about himself. It is never used in recounting a personal experience; for that it is much too alienating a term.

It is very unfortunate that a term such as "parapraxis" interferes with a true appreciation of what Freud called the psychopathology of everyday life, because this book is in many ways his most accessible work and the best introduction to psychoanalysis. Freud thought so himself; he devoted the first four chapters of his *Introductory Lectures on Psychoanalysis* to the discussion of *Fehlleistungen*. Faulty achievements are important for gaining a basic understanding of what psychoanalysis is all about because they elucidate types of behavior with which we are all familiar from our own experiences. They impress on us that psychoanalysis applies to us.

XIII

"Parapraxis" is by no means a unique example of a mistranslation of Freud's carefully chosen language into gobbledygook English. What American psychoanalysts refer to as "cathexis" is designated in German by the verb *besetzen* and the noun *Besetzung*. These two words, in the sense in which Freud used them, simply mean "to occupy" and "occupation." Freud gave these terms a special meaning within his system to indicate that something—an idea, a person, an object—is being or has been invested with a certain amount of psychic energy, which has then become fixated there. One of the common uses of *Besetzung* which made it suitable for Freud's purpose is in the sense of occupation by the military; that is, by a strong power or force.

Freud shunned arcane technical terms whenever he could, not just because using them was bad style but also because the essence of psychoanalysis is to make the unknown known, to make hidden ideas accessible to common understanding. A foreign word gives one the impression that it must refer to some alien matter, outside the realm of one's normal experience. On reading about cathexis, one gets the impression that this must be one of those strange psychological mechanisms that may occur in others, but one cannot be quite sure, because the word does not permit one to find in oneself a feeling for what it means. One rightly thinks that if the word and what it signifies pertained to oneself, or to things that happen in everybody's life, then there would be a word available in the language one normally uses.

In most cases, there were good words readily available to say in English what Freud said in German, if only his translators had been content to use them. One of the definitions both *Webster's* and the OED give for the English verb "to invest" is "to furnish with power, privilege, or authority," and that is exactly what happens when psychic energy becomes fixated to something: that something then exercises power (the energy invested in it) and authority over the rest of our psychic functioning. The English phrase "to charge with energy" would perhaps do as well. In a footnote in the *Standard Edition*, Strachey writes, "The German word [for cathexis] is one in ordinary use, and, among many other senses, might have some such meaning as 'occupation' or 'filling.' Freud, who disliked unnecessary technical terms, was unhappy when in 1922 the present editor, in the supposed interests of clarity, introduced the invented word 'cathexis' (from the Greek . . . *catechein*, to occupy) as a translation."

It would admittedly be difficult to find a single English word to express what Freud had in mind with *Schaulust*—a term that combines the German word for lust, or sexual desire, with that for looking, viewing, or contemplating—but a phrase on the order of "the sexual pleasure in looking" would make his meaning clear; or, since "lust" is a near-equivalent of the German *Lust* and has the further advantage that it can be used both as a noun and as a verb, it might be preferable to "sexual pleasure." In either case, the reader would know immediately what is meant. Since we have all repeatedly experienced great pleasure in watching something, in taking it in with our eyes, and have occasionally been ashamed of doing so, or even been afraid to look, although we wished to see, it would be easy to have both a direct intellectual and an emotional understanding of Freud's concept. In any case, the monstrosity contrived by Freud's translators and perpetuated in the *Standard Edition* —"scopophilia"—certainly conveys nothing at all.

Freud's translators did not always rely on strange Greek words for making it difficult to gain an understanding of what he had in mind, or for making it seem that psychoanalysis deals with esoteric behavioral phenomena rather than with everyday events and processes and ordinary human beings. The translators did this even when they employed common English expressions. Where Freud used the word *Abwehr* it is translated as "defense," despite the fact that "defense" has an exact German equivalent, *Verteidigung*. There are good reasons why Freud chose *Abwehr* rather than *Verteidigung*. When we think or speak of defense, an external enemy comes immediately to mind—someone or something that we must defend ourselves against. It does not occur to us at first that we have to defend ourselves against ourselves. "Defense" and "defender" are terms commonly used in courts of law, as are the German words *Verteidigung* and *Verteidiger*; from this usage alone we get the feeling that it is an external enemy against whom we defend ourselves, or against whom we are defended by a third person. *Abwehr* is a common German word that is best translated as "parrying" or "warding off." James Strachey recognized that "defense" was a questionable translation; in the "Notes on Some Technical Terms Whose Translation Calls for Comment" which he added to his General Preface to the *Stan-*

dard Edition, he writes: "I have accepted the established translation 'defence,' though it gives a more passive impression than the German. The true sense is given better by 'to fend off.' "

Webster's first definition of "defense" is "the act or power of defending," and it says about "defend" that the word "implies an active effort to repel an actual attack or invasion." "To fend off" is defined as "to ward off, parry," but since etymologically the word "fend" has the same root as "defend" and "defense," not much seems to be gained from using it. The verb "parry," by contrast, has a quite different etymological derivation and is defined as "to ward off or deflect, to turn aside as by a clever or evasive reply or remark." This is closest to what Freud had in mind, because the phenomenon to which he referred consists of clever psychological measures taken to deflect or ward off unconscious content we wish to evade. *Webster's* definitions of "defense" and "defend" do not suggest the possibility of using these terms to describe inner psychological processes. There is in fact no defense possible against ourselves, even though there are in each of us inner processes, feelings, unconscious thoughts, and so on, which we strongly wish to protect ourselves against. The translation of *Abwehr* as "defense" reflects an effort to view as external, or as a response to external events, something that is in truth an internal process. What is worst about using the word "defense" is that it permits, even encourages, the impression that inner processes, such as reaction formations or denials, are something alien—something outside oneself. While one may think or wish this were so, the task of psychoanalysis is to show that it is not. Psychoanalysis tries to make us see that what we thought of as something alien that we need to deny or parry is really a very significant part of ourselves, and that it is to our advantage to recognize what it is and to integrate it into our personality.

In Strachey's notes on translations in the General Preface to the *Standard Edition*, he does not discuss *Verdrängung*, a term that is most often translated as "repression." Freud introduced this concept in his paper "*Die Verdrängung*" (1915), where he declared that "its essence consists only of the rebuff or a keeping at a distance from the conscious"—a statement that suggests how *Verdrängung* should have been translated. The important difference between *Verdrängung* and "repression" is that the German word implies an inner urge. *Verdrängung* is derived from the word *Drang*, which is explained in *Duden* by the example "to give in to a strong inner motive." A *Verdrängung* is thus a displacement or dislodgement caused by an inner process. The German word gives no indication in which direction such dislodging or pushing away takes place.

These are probably the reasons why Freud preferred *Verdrängung* to the exact German equivalent of "repression," *Unterdrückung* (literally, "squeezing under"), which indicates that something has been pushed under something else, and which does not carry the connotation of referring to an inner process. Both "repression" and "suppression" (which is also sometimes used as a translation of *Verdrängung*) indicate a direction. Outside of psychoanalytic writings, the words "repression" and "suppression" are used to describe what somebody does to somebody or something else, but not to indicate a personal inner process. *Webster's* offers the examples "to repress a child" and "to suppress a book." Where the OED defines "repression" by means of the example "to hold back a person from action," what is meant is another person, not oneself. *Unterdrückung* has these same meanings and connotations in German. The translation of *Verdrängung* as "repression" makes what happens seem more physical, directed against something outside oneself, than Freud had intended. Correct translations of the noun *Verdrängung* and the verb *verdrängen* would have been "repulsion" and "to repulse." According to the OED, the meaning of "repulsion" is "the action of forcing or driving back or away," and "to repulse" means "to drive or beat back, to repel or ward off, to force back; to repel with denial; to reject, refuse, shut out"—all actions and motivations that are implied in the word Freud selected.

Where Freud speaks of something coming spontaneously to one's mind, something that happens to occur to one, the translators use the incorrect term "free association." This term is incorrect because associations are not "free" but are always conditioned by or related to something; the adjective is misleading. Also, using the technical term "free association" to describe a procedure entails the *a priori* assumption that two or more seemingly entirely disconnected events are indeed fairly closely connected. *Webster's* definition of the verb "associate"—"to join together, connect"— makes this amply clear. In the translators' use of "free association," what ought to be two separate processes—letting something come spontaneously to one's mind, and examining how it may be connected to some immediately preceding stimulus—are merged into one, and it is predicted what the result of this investigation will be.

The German word that has been translated as "free association" is *Einfall*, which means an idea that suddenly happens to come to one's mind; *Einfall* refers to something that is at first impersonal, and conveys the same feeling that is expressed when one says, "It comes to my mind"—a statement in which one connects "it" with one's it, the unconscious from where this idea suddenly emanates. Association, on the other hand, is a conscious process, deliberately engaged in. When a person consciously tries to "free-associate," what he says or does is usually logically connected with the stimulus. For example, when asked to associate to "cold," as likely as not what will come to mind are either opposites ("hot" or "warm") or typical instances in which the word "cold" logically applies ("winter" or "ice" or "freeze"). That is, the response to the stimulus will be intellectually conditioned, since the task of associating is experienced as a demand made of the person's intellect. But the invitation to tell whatever chances to come to mind suggests by its phrasing that the connection between stimulus and association should be not a logical but a chance one. It is characteristic of the often very difficult work of psychoanalysis to try to discover the hidden relations that tie a seemingly inappropriate (i.e., nonlogical) response coming from the unconscious to the stimulus. It then becomes apparent that the stimulus and what "occurred to me, although it doesn't make sense," are in fact closely related because of their emotional connection in the person's life experience. In "free associations" the person's mind is dominant; in "it happens to occur to me" the person's heart has a much better chance to speak.

This is the reason why Freud asked—and why psychoanalysts today ask—"What comes to your mind in connection with that?" ("*Was fällt Ihnen dazu ein?*"). And the answer, when put into words, is "It occurs to me . . ." which clearly refers to the it, from where this new and unexpected idea suddenly and often surprisingly emerges.

XIV

Freud's translators have also used subtler ways of putting a distance between him and the reader. For instance, in the *Standard Edition*, Freud's references to himself sometimes simply disappear. One of many examples of this type of mistranslation is found in Freud's paper "Some Psychological Consequences of the Anatomical Distinction Between the Sexes" (1925), where he writes about a process "which I should like to describe as 'denial' " ("*den ich als 'Verleugnung' bezeichnen möchte*"). This phrase is translated in the *Standard Edition* as "which might be described as 'denial.' " This defective translation impersonally renders a personal statement, and in such transmutations it is the human being who is eliminated, not just Freud the person. Yet psychoanalysis is about nothing except human beings!

The differences between the sexes play an important role in psychoanalytic theory, as they do in all aspects of our lives. In the essay just mentioned, Freud discusses the consequences of the anatomical *differences* between the sexes (". . . *Folgen des Geschlechtsunterschieds*"), but the translators speak instead of a *distinction*. The most common translation of *Unterschied* is "difference," not "distinction." While translation of *Unterschied* as "distinction" is not incorrect, it does not provide a truly accurate rendering of Freud's meaning here. *Webster's* discriminates between "difference" and "distinction" as follows: "different, applied to things which are not alike, implies individuality (three *different* doctors) or contrast; distinct, as applied to two or more things, stresses that each has a different identity and is unmistakably separate from the others." If "difference" indeed stresses contrast and individuality in what is basically likeness (as the example of three different doctors implies), then it is preferable to "distinction" in the context of this essay and its title.

While deeply wrong in a psychological, and particularly in a psychoanalytic sense, translations like this one are at least not blatantly in error on a purely intellectual level. The same cannot be said, of course, of all the mistranslations. Some of the translations are so obviously wrong that it is difficult to understand why they were ever made, and even more difficult to see why they were not corrected long ago. These mistranslations do not necessarily alienate the reader by their strangeness; on the contrary, some of them use very familiar words and are easily understandable. But by saying something quite different from what Freud had in mind, and from what he was talking about in the rest of the article or book at hand, they baffle the reader.

Freud's book *Massenpsychologie und Ich-Analyse* was

written long before Hitler's rise to power, but the events of the 1930s and 1940s and similar events since then have made particularly pertinent Freud's analysis of the psychological factors that explain the fascination dictators exercise over their followers. The title of this book has been translated as *Group Psychology and the Analysis of the Ego*, even though *Masse* has the same meaning as the English word "mass" and "group" is equivalent to the German *Gruppe*. Freud's examples in the book include armies and members of the church —that is, very large numbers of people who do not necessarily know each other and who receive their coherence as a crowd, or mass, only through common acceptance of ideas and leaders. "Mass" is exactly what Freud had in mind; the term is defined in *Webster's* as "a quantity of matter forming a body of indefinite shape and size, usually of relatively large size." In the *Standard Edition* the only explanation we are given for this erroneous translation is in one of Strachey's footnotes: " 'Group' is used throughout this translation as equivalent to the rather more comprehensive German *'Masse.'* The author uses the latter word." No justification is given for considering "group" and "mass" as equivalent terms—which, of course, according to both common usage and the dictionary definitions, they are not. Readers who turn to this book to learn about group psychology will be sorely disappointed. But since the text makes it quite clear that Freud is talking about the psychology of crowd behavior and the phenomena which underly the formation of large masses, the damage may be overcome by the serious reader.

Matters are much more problematic in respect to *Civilization and Its Discontents*, Freud's most important treatise on society. Even a close reading of the English translation of this book does not permit an understanding of some of its central ideas, because faulty translations of certain main concepts persist throughout the text. Freud called the book *Das Unbehagen in der Kultur,* and a correct translation of his title would be *The Uneasiness Inherent in Culture.* The reasons for the mistranslation of this title are incomprehensible. In German, there is a great distinction between the words *Kultur* (culture) and *Zivilisation* (civilization). *Kultur* refers to moral value systems, and to intellectual and esthetic achievements—in short, to what might be called the humanities. *Zivilisation* refers to material and technological accomplishments. When Freud used the word *Kultur,* he had in mind those aspects of our world that he cherished most highly; and, as we know, he was highly critical of many aspects of material and technological civilization. There can be no doubt that the difference between *Kultur* and *Zivilisation* was important to Freud. In his letter to Einstein, published under the title "Why War?," he wrote:

Since time immemorial mankind has been undergoing a process of cultural development. (I know, others prefer to call it a process of civilization.) To this process we owe the best that we have become, and a good part of that from which we suffer. (*Seit unvordenklichen Zeiten zieht sich über die Menschheit der Prozess der Kulturentwicklung. [Ich weiss, andere heissen ihn lieber: Zivilisation.] Diesem Prozess verdanken wir das Beste, was wir geworden sind, und ein gut Teil von dem, woran wir leiden.*)

Unfortunate though the translation of *Kultur* as "civilization" may be, much more serious are the mistranslations of *Unbehagen* (uneasiness) and *in* (the German preposition *in* can be translated as "in" or "within," depending on the context; in order to render Freud's title more idiomatically, I have translated *in* as "inherent in"). The word "and" can and frequently does connect quite different things. The words "in" and "within" clearly indicate that the two words they bind together—and the ideas to which these words refer—are encapsulated to form some kind of unit, often an inseparable one. The title *Das Unbehagen in der Kultur* implies that a certain discomfort is necessarily or unavoidably inherent in culture; the title's accepted English translation in no way conveys this idea. The English title might be acceptable if Freud had called his book *Zivilisation und Ihre Unzufriedenheiten* (a literal translation of the English title) or even *Die Unzufriedenheit mit der Kultur*, since the English word "civilization" does cover a broader spectrum of phenomena than the German *Zivilisation*. As these two translations of the English title into German suggest, the word "discontent" has an exact German equivalent, and it is not *Unbehagen*, the word Freud used, but *Unzufriedenheit*. Unfortunately, *Unbehagen* has no exact equivalent in English; but its meaning is intimated by the fact that *Unbehagen* is the opposite of *Behagen*, which is easily translated into English as "comfort" or "ease." (Freud himself suggested that *Unbehagen* be translated as either "discomfort" or "malaise," but never as "discontent.") "Uneasiness" seems the best translation of *Unbehagen*, because Freud used the word to designate a *feeling*. "Discontent" is an unsatisfactory translation because discontent can be and often is the result of intellectual speculations; one of the definitions of the word given in the OED is "dissatisfaction of mind."

Here, then, in one short title are three erroneous translations that could easily have been avoided—a typical example of the truth of the old adage *Traditore, traduttore*: translators are "traitors" to the ideas of the author, because they lead readers into misconceptions.

In his letter to Einstein, Freud made the important point that we owe to the development of our culture not only the very best that we have become but also a good part of that from which we suffer. To explain why this is so is the purpose of Freud's book *Das Unbehagen in der Kultur*. He shows that this uneasiness, these feelings of malaise, are the price we must pay for enjoying all the great advantages we derive from our culture. He elucidates the valid psychological reasons why culture cannot be had without this uneasiness, and he makes clear that *Unbehagen* is the inescapable concomitant of those sublimations which are necessary for achieving a cultured existence. In complete denial of this idea, Freud's translators have made it easy to believe that civilization and discontent are two separate phenomena. Readers of the English translation, particularly those casual readers who judge the book by its title, might think that Freud was critical of a civilization that brought about discontent with life. They might imagine that they could have civilization without discontent, mistakenly believing that psychoanalysis suggests this is possible and even desirable. Such a notion is childish and narcissistic, completely contrary to what Freud had in mind.

Probably among the worst distortions of Freud's thoughts is the interpretation of narcissism as positive and normal, the appropriate consequence of a natural selfishness. It has been observed lately that the present American culture is essentially narcissistic. Selfishness, concentration on the self, wishing to have one's way at any cost—all narcissistic traits—are everywhere in evidence. It seems that quite a number of Americans, in their efforts to attain the good life, have made themselves their prime love object, advocating self-assertion over concern for others, looking out for Number One. This is directly opposed to Freud's conviction that the good life—or, at least, the best life available to man, the most enjoyable and most meaningful—consists of being able truly to love not oneself but others, and of being able to find meaningful and satisfactory work that will have positive results also for others. Freud evoked the myth of Narcissus to help us understand that egocentricity is undesirable. Without a clear understanding of what this myth implies—that Narcissus' infatuation with himself causes him to destroy himself—one fails to understand why Freud applied the term "narcissistic" to the most primitive stage of human development, the stage in which the utterly helpless infant compensates for his helplessness with a megalomanic self-centeredness. Freud did so to warn us against narcissism, to warn us of the destructive consequences of remaining fixated on a caring only for oneself. He knew that caring only for oneself is self-defeating, that it alienates one from others and from the real world, and, eventually, from oneself, too. Narcissus, who looked only at his own reflection, lost touch with humanity, even his own. According to psychoanalytic theory, amply supported by the findings of its practice, loving oneself too much results in emotional starvation. What the myth symbolically represents as Narcissus drowning in his own image is in actuality the emotional deadness of the narcissistic person. Narcissism leads to a shallow, meaningless life, devoid of close, reciprocal, mutually satisfying and enriching relations with others, which represent the best life has to offer.

XV

St. Jerome remarked about some translations of the Bible that they are not versions but, rather, perversions of the original. The same could be said of the way many psychoanalytic concepts have been translated into English. Particularly regrettable is the translation of *Trieb* as "instinct," because the concept it denotes has such an important role in the Freudian system. This is one of the few translations about which James Strachey felt uneasy enough to discuss it at some length in his notes for the *Standard Edition*:

> "*Trieb.*" "*Instinct.*" My choice of this rendering has been attacked in some quarters with considerable, but, I think, mistaken severity. The term almost invariably proposed by critics as an alternative is "drive." There are several objections to this. First, I should like to remark that "drive," used in this sense, is not an English word. . . . The critics obviously choose it because of its superficial resemblance to the German "*Trieb,*" and I suspect that the majority of

them are in fact influenced by a native or early familiarity with the German language. . . . [In] my choice of "instinct" . . . the only slight complication is that in some half-dozen instances Freud himself uses the German "*Instinkt*," always, perhaps, in the sense of instinct in animals.

This is hardly a "slight complication." Freud used the German word *Instinkt* when it seemed appropriate to him —to refer to the inborn instincts of animals—and he shunned it when he was speaking of human beings. Since Freud made a clear distinction between what he had in mind when he spoke of instincts and what he had in mind when he spoke of *Triebe*, the importance of retaining the distinction seems obvious. The notion that "drive" is not an English noun is not very convincing, coming from translators who have created such terms as "parapraxis" and "scopophilia." Its obvious merit can be seen in the fact that in recent years it has become standard American usage. According to *Webster's*, "drive" is both a noun and a verb. As a noun it means, in general, "the power or energy to get things done; enthusiastic or aggressive vigor"; and in psychology, in particular, "any of the basic biological impulses or urges, such as self-preservation, hunger, sex, etc."—exactly what Freud meant by *Trieb*. As a matter of fact, when we say that we are driven by ambition or fear we are using a verb form of "drive" to denote inner propulsion by a force corresponding to Freud's *Trieb*. It would never occur to us to refer to "instinct" in such contexts. It can be argued that "impulse" is a better rendering than "instinct" for *Trieb*. *Webster's* defines "impulse" as "an impelling force; a sudden inclination to act, without conscious thought; a motive or tendency coming from within." It would be difficult to come closer to Freud's meaning, and, indeed, in French editions of his works *Trieb* is translated as *pulsion*. And "impulse" has the added advantage of offering the adjective "impulsive."

In translating the title of Freud's important paper *"Triebe und Triebschicksale"* (1915), the translators have made two grievous mistakes. Not only have they rendered *Triebe* as "instincts" but they have replaced *Schicksale* ("fates," "destinies") with "vicissitudes." The title is given in the *Standard Edition* as "Instincts and Their Vicissitudes." "Fate" is a word that we readily apply to ourselves and to other human beings when we speak of what happens to us during a lifetime. Freud used this word to bring what he was talking about closer to us and the way we experience life. We do not apply the term "vicissitude" to ourselves or to the course of events that shape our lives; it is, as *Webster's* declares it to be, a bookish term. It evokes no emotional reaction. In fact, "vicissitude" is a term that is readily used to describe nonhuman occurrences; the OED gives the example "the vicissitude of tides." It is true that both "fate" and "destiny" carry the implication of inevitability, which neither the German *Schicksale* nor the English "vicissitudes" does. And Freud certainly did not mean that there is any inevitability inherent in the changes our inner drives are subject to. But if the translators rejected "fate" because of its implication of immutability, they could have used "change" or "mutability" instead. They could, for example, have translated the title as "Drives and Their Mutability."

In this paper, Freud set down his belief that impulses or

drives can be changed in various ways: into their opposites; directed against the person himself; or suppressed; or sublimated. "Instincts" is the wrong word for what Freud had in mind precisely because instincts are inborn, unconscious, and basically unalterable. *Webster's* defines "instinct" as "an inborn tendency to behave in ways characteristic of a species, an unacquired mode of response to stimuli." The OED calls "instinct" an "innate propensity in organized beings (especially in the lower animals), varying with the species, and manifesting itself in acts which appear to be rational, but are performed without conscious adaptation of means to ends." Freud never believed that the most important aspects of our behavior are determined by our instincts and are therefore beyond the reach of our influence. (If they were psychoanalytic therapy would be an impossibility.) As he wrote in a famous passage in the *New Introductory Lectures*, the purpose of psychoanalysis is "to strengthen the I, to make it more independent of the above-I, to widen its field of perception and to extend its organization so that it can appropriate to itself new portions of the it," and he added "Where it was, there should become I." Psychoanalysis attempts to demonstrate that our most basic motives *are* subject to conscious recognition and deliberate alteration. If "I" am driven by fear or ambition or greed, "I" can do something about it. Men and women, unlike animals, can change themselves in significant ways.

In no respect has the rendering of *Trieb* as "instinct" done more harm to the understanding of psychoanalysis than in its use in connection with the "death instinct." Indeed, there would be no point to a psychoanalysis that posited a death instinct, and for this reason American psycho analysis rightly distances itself from the idea of a death instinct. But Freud never spoke of a death instinct—only of a mostly unconscious drive or impulse that provokes us to aggressive, destructive, and self-destructive actions. Some of us are certainly driven toward death—our own death or death inflicted on others. Otherwise, how could one explain suicides that are not due to an incurable sickness or some similar cause—suicides by affluent American adolescents, for example? Without the concept of a death drive, some events of recent history—German history in particular—are incomprehensible. To reject the idea of the death impulse is to reduce Freud's dualistic system—according to which in our soul a passionate struggle raging between two contrary impulses determines what we feel and do, and which in large measure explains the difficulties from which we suffer—to a monistic system capable of supporting only the most placid view of our inner life.

Freud took care to emphasize the conflicts within the soul, and their consequences for an individual: how he could live well with himself despite these conflicts—or possibly because of them, since they also make for the richness of his inner life. If we disregard what he referred to, in *Civilization and Its Discontents*, as the battle of "the two 'Heavenly Powers' "—of "eternal Eros" against "his equally eternal opponent [Thanatos]"—then the crucial problem facing us is no longer how to manage our inner conflicts and contradictions (that is, how to get along with ourselves) but merely how to get along. That problem was of no interest whatever to Freud. Such simplification and reductionism opened the door to the interpretation of Freud's system as advocating 'adjustment"—something that Freud never advocated—

and to a disregard of his pessimistic and tragic view of life and its replacement by a pragmatic meliorism.

With the mistranslation of Freud's thoughts to make them fit better into a behavioristic frame of reference—a frame of reference completely alien to psychoanalysis—it is understandable that in the English-speaking world his concepts were not only examined in this light but found wanting. If behavioristic studies could prove Freud right, his would no longer be an introspective psychology that tries to elucidate the darkest recesses of the soul—the forces least accessible to our observation. Behaviorism concentrates on what can be seen from the outside, what can be studied objectively by an uninvolved observer, what can be replicated and assigned numerical values. Psychoanalysis is concerned with what is unique to a person's life—with his unique life history, which makes him different from all other people—and it is an approach diametrically opposed to behaviorism. All this might have been obvious if Freud's references to man's soul and the conflicts within it had been retained in the English translation of his writings. Our everyday experiences would have made it easy for us to accept the idea that much of man's behavior is most readily explained by the assumption that very strong destructive impulses dwell in all of us. Because in translation Freud's statements about these aggressive impulses seem to show them as reflections or consequences of a "death instinct," his critics have found it easy to prove those statements wrong. As happened so often during his lifetime, he has continued since his death to be accused and found guilty of doctrines he never held.

For Freud, the I was a sphere of tragic conflict. From the moment we are born until the moment we die, Eros and Thanatos struggle for dominance in shaping our lives, and make it difficult for us to be at peace with ourselves for anything but short periods. Freud's system in its later development establishes the concept of an eternal struggle between the life and death drives in us and recognizes the need to help the life drive prevent the death drive from damaging us. It is this struggle which makes emotional richness possible; which explains the multifarious nature of a man's life; which makes alike for depression and elation; which gives life its deepest meaning.

To imagine, as many Americans do, that psychoanalysis makes it possible to build a satisfying life on a belief in the sexual, or life, drive alone is to misunderstand Freud completely. Just as an exclusive preoccupation with the death drive would make us morbidly depressed and ineffective, an exclusive preoccupation with the sexual, or life, drive can only lead to a shallow, narcissistic existence, because it evades reality and robs life of what makes every moment of it uniquely significant—the fact that it might be our last one.

The sexual drive presses for immediate satisfaction; it neither knows nor cares for the future. Eros and Psyche do. Being aware of the tragic limits placed on our existence by our mortality and our destructiveness induces us to wish to see life continue after us. Awareness of the dark aspects of life makes us keenly conscious of the need to secure a better life for those we love, and for those who come after us—not only our own children but the next generation as a whole. It was our love for others, and our concern for the future of those we love, that Freud had in mind when he spoke of "eternal Eros." The love for others—the working of eternal Eros—finds its expression in the relations we f rm with those who are important to us and in what we do to make a better life, a better world for them. The goal is not an impossible utopia, where there will no longer be any uneasiness or discomfort inherent in culture, but a culture that will ever better justify the price of uneasiness which we pay for the advantages it confers on us. The good life, in Freud's view, is one that is full of meaning through the lasting, sustaining, mutually gratifying relations we are able to establish with those we love, and through the satisfaction we derive from knowing that we are engaged in work that helps us and others to have a better life. A good life denies neither its real and often painful difficulties nor the dark aspects of our psyche; rather, it is a life in which our hardships are not permitted to engulf us in despair, and our dark impulses are not allowed to draw us into their chaotic and often destructive orbit.

Through recognizing the true nature of our unconscious, and the role it plays in our psyche, we may achieve an existence in which Eros, the life drive, maintains its ascendancy over everything within us that is chaotic, irrational, and destructive—in short, over the consequences of what Freud called the death drive, to which we are also heir. A reasonable dominance of our I over our it and above-I—this was Freud's goal for all of us. Through his work and his writings, he strove to make a rational and feeling life possible. It would be to our immense advantage to heed these lessons he tried to teach us.

In his last great theoretical paper on psychoanalysis,

"Analysis Terminable and Interminable" (1937), Freud wrote, "There can be no question of an antithesis between an optimistic and a pessimistic theory of life; only the simultaneous working together and against each other of both primordial drives, of Eros and the death drive, can explain the colorfulness of life, never the one or the other all by itself." Poets express the same insight in their own language. Faulkner, in the speech he gave on accepting the Nobel Prize, said, "The problems of the human heart in conflict with itself . . . alone can make good writing." Not only good writing, he might have added, but all else that is best in man.

The conflict in our soul between Eros and Thanatos can bring forth the worst and the very best in our thoughts and actions. Recognition of the worst possibilities—the destruction of all mankind—led Freud to his tragic view of life. But the best possibilities inherent in our soul sustained him even in deepest adversity, and made his life not just bearable but worthwhile and, at times, truly satisfying. Freud knew few periods of complete ease in his life. That he, like all sensitive human beings, had to suffer from feelings of uneasiness was something he recognized and accepted as but a small price to pay for being able to enjoy the advantages of the culture that is man's highest achievement.

We should not see such malaise as anything unusual; Goethe said that in seventy-five years he had experienced barely four weeks of being truly at ease. An inescapable sadness is part of the life of any reflective person, but it is only part—by no means all—of living. In the end, Thanatos wins, but as long as there is life in us we can keep Eros victorious over Thanatos. This we must do if we wish to live well. The prime requirement for this is that we love well and live so that we are well loved by those who are most important to us. If we do, then Eros prevails and Psyche rejoices.

We owe much to those before us and around us who created our humanity through the elevating insights and cultural achievements that are our pride, and make life worth all its pains; and we must recognize, with Freud, what those creators of our humanity did not deny but accepted and endured in the realization that only in conflict with itself can the human heart (as Faulkner said) or the human soul (as Freud would have said) attain what is best in life.

FOR THE BEST IN PAPERBACKS, LOOK FOR THE 🐧

In every corner of the world, on every subject under the sun, Penguin represents quality and variety – the very best in publishing today.

For complete information about books available from Penguin – including Puffins, Penguin Classics and Arkana – and how to order them, write to us at the appropriate address below. Please note that for copyright reasons the selection of books varies from country to country.

In the United Kingdom: Please write to *Dept E.P., Penguin Books Ltd, Harmondsworth, Middlesex, UB7 0DA.*

If you have any difficulty in obtaining a title, please send your order with the correct money, plus ten per cent for postage and packaging, to *PO Box No 11, West Drayton, Middlesex*

In the United States: Please write to *Dept BA, Penguin, 299 Murray Hill Parkway, East Rutherford, New Jersey 07073*

In Canada: Please write to *Penguin Books Canada Ltd, 2801 John Street, Markham, Ontario L3R 1B4*

In Australia: Please write to the *Marketing Department, Penguin Books Australia Ltd, P.O. Box 257, Ringwood, Victoria 3134*

In New Zealand: Please write to the *Marketing Department, Penguin Books (NZ) Ltd, Private Bag, Takapuna, Auckland 9*

In India: Please write to *Penguin Overseas Ltd, 706 Eros Apartments, 56 Nehru Place, New Delhi, 110019*

In the Netherlands: Please write to *Penguin Books Netherlands B.V., Postbus 195, NL–1380AD Weesp*

In West Germany: Please write to *Penguin Books Ltd, Friedrichstrasse 10–12, D–6000 Frankfurt/Main 1*

In Spain: Please write to *Longman Penguin España, Calle San Nicolas 15, E–28013 Madrid*

In Italy: Please write to *Penguin Italia s.r.l., Via Como 4, I-20096 Pioltello (Milano)*

In France: Please write to *Penguin Books Ltd, 39 Rue de Montmorency, F-75003 Paris*

In Japan: Please write to *Longman Penguin Japan Co Ltd, Yamaguchi Building, 2-12-9 Kanda Jimbocho, Chiyoda-Ku, Tokyo 101*

PENGUIN PSYCHOLOGY

Introduction to Jung's Psychology Frieda Fordham

'She has delivered a fair and simple account of the main aspects of my psychological work. I am indebted to her for this admirable piece of work' – C. G. Jung in the Foreword

Child Care and the Growth of Love John Bowlby

His classic 'summary of evidence of the effects upon children of lack of personal attention ... it presents to administrators, social workers, teachers and doctors a reminder of the significance of the family' – *The Times*

The Anatomy of Human Destructiveness Erich Fromm

What makes men kill? How can we explain man's lust for cruelty and destruction? 'If any single book could bring mankind to its senses, this book might qualify for that miracle' – Lewis Mumford

Sanity, Madness and the Family R. D. Laing and A. Esterson

Schizophrenia: fact or fiction? Certainly not fact, according to the authors of this controversial book. Suggesting that some forms of madness may be largely social creations, *Sanity, Madness and the Family* demands to be taken very seriously indeed.

The Social Psychology of Work Michael Argyle

Both popular and scholarly, Michael Argyle's classic account of the social factors influencing our experience of work examines every area of working life – and throws constructive light on potential problems.

Check Your Own I.Q. H. J. Eysenck

The sequel to his controversial bestseller, containing five new standard (omnibus) tests and three specifically designed tests for verbal, numerical and visual–spatial ability.

BY THE SAME AUTHOR

The Informed Heart

A study of the psychological consequences of living under extreme fear and terror.

Bruno Bettelheim spent a year in the concentration camps of Dachau and Buchenwald. In order to keep alive and remain human, he began to analyse the behaviour of those around him. This book contains the insights he obtained into how people react to extreme conditions – insights which later proved vital in his world-famous work with autistic children.

'None of the numerous novels or poems that have taken on the dread theme of the concentration camps rival the truth, the controlled poetic mercy of Bruno Bettelheim's factual analysis' – George Steiner

The Uses of Enchantment

The meaning and importance of fairy tales.

Dr Bettelheim wrote this book to help adults become aware of the irreplaceable importance of fairy tales. By revealing the true content of such stories, he shows how children may make use of them to cope with their baffling emotions, whether they be feelings of smallness and helplessness or the anxieties the child feels about strangers and the mysteries of the outside world. Taking the best-known stories in turn, he demonstrates how they work, consciously or unconsciously, to support and free the child.

'Bruno Bettelheim's tour of fairy stories, with all their psychoanalytic connotations brought out into the open, is a feast of understanding' – Richard Bourne in *New Society*

The Uses of Enchantment was awarded the Critics' Choice Prize for the best work of criticism published in the United States in 1976 and the National Book Award in 1977.